# THE
# YOUNG PEOPLE'S
# ATLAS
## OF THE
# UNITED STATES

KINGFISHER
LONDON & NEW YORK

Copyright © 2004 by Kingfisher
Published in the United States by Kingfisher,
175 Fifth Ave., New York, NY 10010
Kingfisher is an imprint of Macmillan Children's Books, London.
All rights reserved.

Distributed in the U.S. by Macmillan, 175 Fifth Ave., New York, NY 10010
Distributed in Canada by H.B. Fenn and Company Ltd., 34 Nixon Road, Bolton, Ontario L7E 1W2

Library of Congress Cataloging-in-Publication Data
Harrison, James
The young people's atlas of the United States/James Harrison,
Eleanor Van Zandt.—New ed. 1st American ed.
p. cm.
Includes index
Summary: An illustrated atlas of the United States including relief
maps of every state, region, and territory with information about
major cities, geography, industry, agriculture, history and people
1. United States—Maps for children. [1. United States—Maps.
2. Atlases.] I. Van Zandt, Eleanor. II. Title. III. Title: Atlas
of the United States
B1200.H39  1996  <G&M>
912. 73—dc20    96-14548   CIP MAP AC

ISBN: 978-0-7534-5022-2

Kingfisher books are available for special promotions and premiums. For details contact:
Special Markets Department, Macmillan, 175 Fifth Avenue, New York, NY 10010.

For more information, please visit www.kingfisherpublications.com

Printed in Taiwan
10 9 8 7 6
6TR/0709/SAP/RNB/120MA/F

# THE
# YOUNG PEOPLE'S
# ATLAS
## OF THE
# UNITED STATES

James Harrison
Eleanor Van Zandt
Consultant: Professor Jack Zevin

KINGFISHER

NEW YORK

# CONTENTS

## FEATURES OF THIS BOOK

**STATE NICKNAME**

**THE TEXT** for each state is full of information. It will give you a clear profile of the state including important facts about its history, economy, and natural features.

**FACT BOXES,** decorated with the state flag, appear throughout the atlas. They include data on the state's capital, area, population, largest cities, chief rivers, state motto, and state song.

**PERSONALITIES,** including well-known Americans from many fields, are highlighted for many of the states with which they are particularly associated.

**STATE SYMBOLS.** Every state has its own bird, tree, and flower emblems. There are beautifully illustrated in full color and clearly labeled in every state spread.

**PHOTOGRAPHS.** Full-color photographs illustrate every page. These depict examples of the state's culture, people, cities, and natural landscape.

**BOXED TEXT** highlights important or special features and is illustrated with a color photograph.

**LOCATION MAP.** Each state has a location map so that you can see at a glance where it is situated.

**RELIEF MAPS** of each state show: contiguous states, major towns and cities, state capitals, national parks, major rivers, and interstate highways. Capitals are marked with a star and cities with a population of over 250,000 are in bold type Mountains are shown in relief. Dry areas are shown in shades of brown. Other areas are forests or grassland.

# INTRODUCTION

THE YOUNG PEOPLE'S ATLAS OF THE UNITED STATES invites you to take a tour of a country that is one of the world's largest, wealthiest, and most geographically exciting areas. Explore the variety of landscapes and peoples that live in the United States, and discover some of its natural beauties and cultural symbols. Find out how the ecology of a state and a region influences its history, character, products, and pastimes.

Don't think of this Altas as merely a collection of maps, but as a guide to those features and people who have shaped the land and used its resources. Decide how the rivers and mountains, plains and valleys, deserts and forests of the United States have sometimes aided, and other times slowed, economic and political development.

Collect information about climate and weather, geology and geography, plants and animals, cities and towns, industries and agriculture for each state, region, and the nation as a whole. Pick out a favorite state and learn more about it. Choose a place you would most like to visit. Imagine yourself discovering new territory ... but remember that someone may have been there before you!

Travel through each state of the Union. Put groups of states together into regions. Then view the states and regions as a single, connected whole ... one nation with a history that might be described as always changing. Change and movement have characterized the United States from the time of its original peoples, the Native American groups, through exploration by European explorers and a revolutionary birth and Civil War ordeal, to its present status as a superpower in world affairs.

Change has also brought about many problems, and you will learn about some of the important ones in this Atlas. The wonders of nature that the United States contains have often been wisely set aside in national parks and forests. But the progress of technology and industry that have provided a high standard of living have also sometimes damaged the environment through pollution and the destruction of habitats. The many immigrants and pioneers who have contributed to the rich culture of the United States have also sometimes clashed with those who went before them, or with each other. Native Americans, African Americans, those of different religions or ethnic groups have often had to struggle to take advantage of the society's wealth and power.

However, problems and all, the story of the fifty states tells about a land of dramatic scenery and plentiful resources. In the cities and towns, suburbs and farms of the United States live millions of people descended from immigrants who came from other lands: Africa, Asia, Europe, and Latin America. All of these form a people who have bonded with their new land, and who share its advantages and its problems.

Often, the face of the earth has been altered to serve human needs through the building of dams, canals, harbors, bridges, and monuments. At other times, areas have been set aside for their beauty, to preserve unique plant and animal life, or to provide for human recreation. Are there any natural places described in this Atlas that you would especially like to see? Are there any human creations or works that you think are amazing? Are there any individuals or peoples that you find particularly interesting? Take us up on our invitation to use this Atlas as a way of exploring the great and fascinating country that is the United States of America.

Professor Jack Zevin
Queens College, City University of New York

# THE UNITED STATES

The United States of America is located (apart from Hawaii) on the continent of North America, which it shares with Canada, Mexico, and the countries of Central America. Often, however, the name "North America" is applied just to Canada and the United States, to distinguish them from their Spanish-speaking neighbors to the south. The name "America" is also commonly used to mean the United States.

The United States includes the 50 states plus the District of Columbia, or Washington, the capital, which is a self-governing city. You will sometimes find the terms "the nation" or "the Union" used to mean the United States (although during the Civil War the "Union" meant the North, as opposed to the Confederacy of southern states).

To refer to the 48 states that touch each other (that is, excluding Hawaii and Alaska) the term "continental United States" is normally used. You will also sometimes find these states called the "contiguous states." The continental United States is bordered on the north by Canada, which is larger in size by 230,230 square miles (596,296 sq. km); on the south by Mexico and the Gulf of Mexico; on the east by the Atlantic Ocean; and on the west by the Pacific. The United States has a number of possessions, including the Commonwealth of Puerto Rico and various Pacific islands.

△ Based on the colors of the Great Seal, it is believed that red, white, and blue have special significance for the U.S. Red stands for courage, white for purity, and blue for justice. The 13 stripes are for the original 13 colonies, and the stars stand for the number of states.

◁ A traditional sled crosses the frozen tundra of the northernmost state, Alaska. The state has a vast wealth of natural resources.

◁ The volcanic islands of Hawaii form the farthest western extent of the United States.

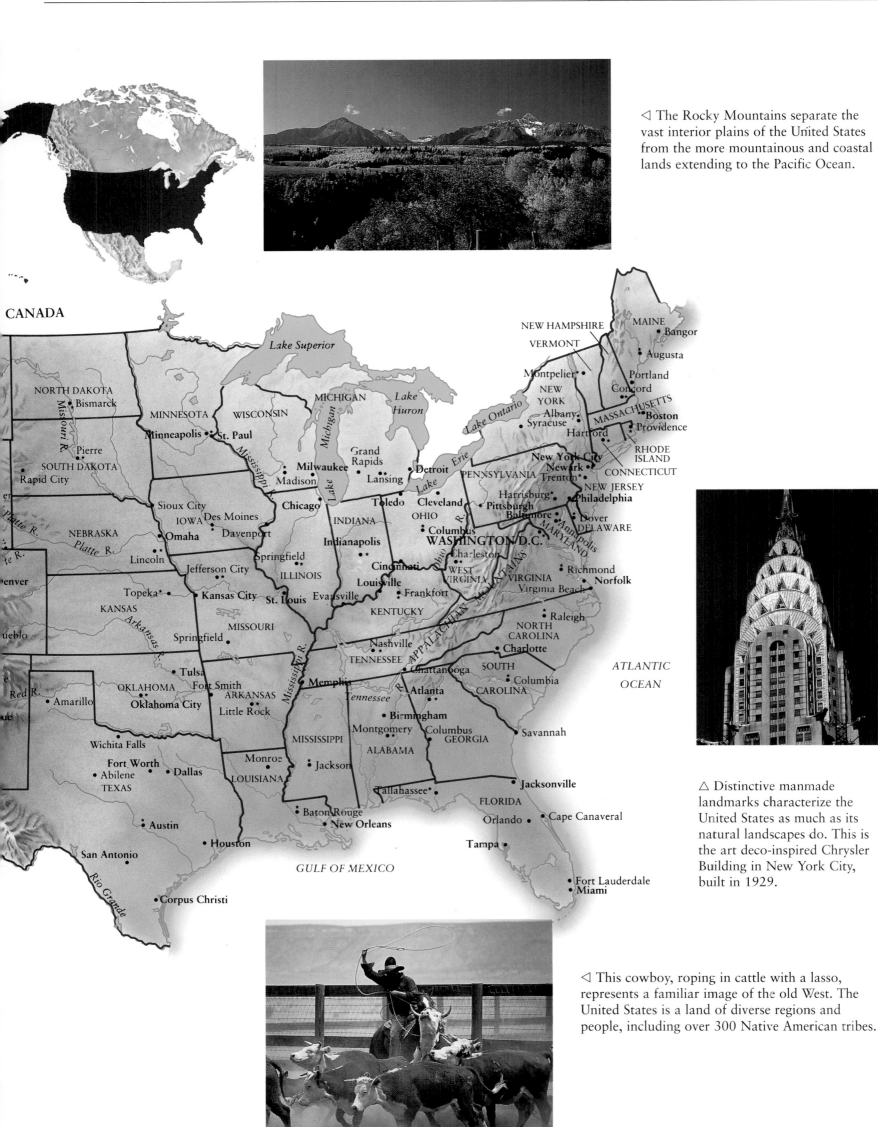

◁ The Rocky Mountains separate the vast interior plains of the United States from the more mountainous and coastal lands extending to the Pacific Ocean.

CANADA

Lake Superior

NORTH DAKOTA
• Bismarck
Missouri R.
MINNESOTA
WISCONSIN
MICHIGAN
Lake Huron
NEW HAMPSHIRE
VERMONT
MAINE
• Bangor
• Augusta

• Pierre
SOUTH DAKOTA
Rapid City
Minneapolis • • St. Paul
Mississippi R.
Lake Michigan
Grand Rapids
Montpelier
NEW YORK
Portland
Concord
• Albany
Syracuse
MASSACHUSETTS
• Boston
• Providence

Platte R.
Sioux City
IOWA Des Moines
• Milwaukee
Madison
• Lansing
Lake Ontario
Lake Erie
Detroit
Cleveland
PENNSYLVANIA
New York City
Newark
Trenton
Hartford
RHODE ISLAND
CONNECTICUT

NEBRASKA
Platte R.
• Omaha
Davenport
Chicago
INDIANA
Toledo
OHIO
Harrisburg
Pittsburgh
Philadelphia
NEW JERSEY

Lincoln
Jefferson City
Springfield
ILLINOIS
Indianapolis
Cincinnati
Ohio R.
Columbus
WASHINGTON D.C.
Baltimore
Annapolis
Dover
DELAWARE
MARYLAND

Topeka
Kansas City
St. Louis
Evansville
Louisville
Frankfort
Charleston
WEST VIRGINIA
VIRGINIA
Richmond
Norfolk
Virginia Beach

KANSAS
Arkansas R.
Springfield
MISSOURI
KENTUCKY
APPALACHIAN MOUNTAINS
Raleigh
NORTH CAROLINA

ueblo
enver
Red R.
ue

Tulsa
OKLAHOMA Fort Smith
Oklahoma City
ARKANSAS
Little Rock
Nashville
TENNESSEE
Tennessee R.
Memphis
Chattanooga
Atlanta
SOUTH CAROLINA
Charlotte
Columbia
ATLANTIC OCEAN

Amarillo
Wichita Falls
Fort Worth
Abilene
Dallas
TEXAS
MISSISSIPPI
Monroe
LOUISIANA
Jackson
Montgomery
Birmingham
ALABAMA
Columbus
GEORGIA
Savannah

San Antonio
Austin
Houston
Rio Grande
Baton Rouge
New Orleans
Tallahassee
Jacksonville
FLORIDA
Orlando
Cape Canaveral
Tampa

Corpus Christi
GULF OF MEXICO
Fort Lauderdale
Miami

△ Distinctive manmade landmarks characterize the United States as much as its natural landscapes do. This is the art deco-inspired Chrysler Building in New York City, built in 1929.

◁ This cowboy, roping in cattle with a lasso, represents a familiar image of the old West. The United States is a land of diverse regions and people, including over 300 Native American tribes.

# THE NORTHEASTERN STATES

The Northeastern region of the United States includes the Middle Atlantic states of New York, New Jersey, and Pennsylvania, and the six New England states: Maine, Massachusetts, New Hampshire, Vermont, Rhode Island, and Connecticut. The dominant physical feature of the Northeast is the Appalachian Mountains—a 1,600-mile (2,575-km) long crescent of mountains stretching from the St. Lawrence Valley in Canada down to northern Alabama. They are comprised of many smaller ranges, including the Green Mountains of Vermont, the White Mountains of New Hampshire, the Alleghenies of Pennsylvania, and the Adirondacks and Catskills of New York. The Northeast has a varied coastline, ranging from the sandy beaches of New Jersey to the rocky shores of Maine.

The name "New England" was given to this extreme northeast area by Captain John Smith, who explored its coast in 1614. In some ways the land does resemble England, and because the first colonists here were nearly all English, there are also many English place names, such as Plymouth and Manchester.

A little farther south, other nations colonized this region—the Dutch in what is now New York and the Germans and Swedes in Pennsylvania—along with many English as well. In addition to farming, these northeastern settlers established industries, such as fishing, whaling, and shipbuilding. They founded many towns, some of which now rank among the nation's most important cities, such as Boston, Philadelphia, and New York. There are many historic sites in the Northeast, especially from the Colonial and Revolutionary War periods.

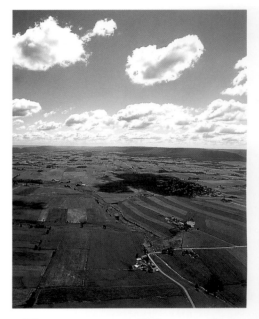

△ There are many small farms on the fertile plains of the Northeast, although agriculture is less important in the region than manufacturing or commerce.

◁ Many of the first New England settlers were Puritans, who practiced a simple way of life. Today some religious sects pursue time-honored lifestyles, such as this farmer with his plow and horses.

▷ White-painted, clapboard churches and houses dot the gently rolling, tree-lined Vermont landscape, which bursts into red and gold in the fall.

◁ Religious freedom was the chief driving force for the first immigrants to the Northeast. Several of the early colonies were governed by religious leaders, and churches such as this were the focal point of the community.

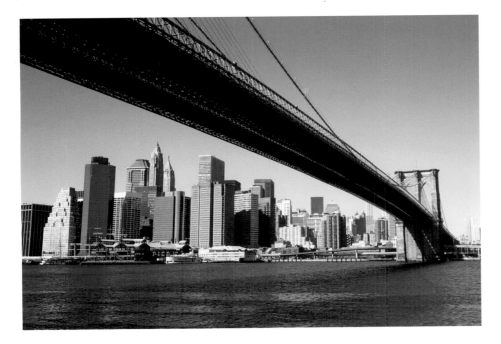

△ The Northeast is steeped in the heritage of the Revolutionary War. It was here that the fighting began between American colonists and British troops. Many important events of the war are commemorated in this region.

◁ New York City is the largest city in the United States and is the country's commercial and cultural "nerve center." It has a thriving port, the busiest in the region, and boasts many famous skyscrapers.

9

# THE SOUTHERN STATES

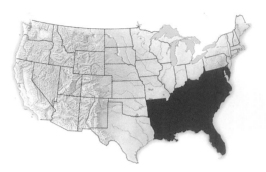

The South is a large region of great geographical variety. Parts of it are mountainous, crossed by the lower end of the Appalachian Mountains, including the Blue Ridge and Great Smoky ranges. Although relatively low, compared to the Rockies, for example, these mountains were, in earlier times, a barrier against westward migration.

The humid, subtropical southern lowlands contain many swamps, such as the Dismal Swamp of Virginia and North Carolina, the Louisiana bayous, and the Florida Everglades. Some of these marshy areas, once dangerous places teeming with disease-bearing mosquitoes, are now important wildlife reserves.

The warm climate and fertile soil of the southern plateaus are ideal for the cultivation of many crops, notably tobacco and cotton. It was the mainly cotton-based economy of the South, dominated by large plantations and run by slave labor, that led to the Civil War in 1861. Eleven Southern states, insisting on their right to maintain slavery against growing opposition from the North, seceded from the Union and formed the Confederate States of America. Only after four years of bitter fighting was the Union restored and slavery finally abolished. The South bears many marks of that struggle, in the form of memorials, statues, cemeteries, and battlefields.

But although the South is a strongly tradition-conscious region, it is an increasingly progressive one, with many high-tech industries located there. The nation's capital, Washington, D.C. (District of Columbia), is also located in the South, between Maryland and Virginia.

△ Many of the grand antebellum (pre-Civil War) mansions of the plantation owners are restored and open to the public. This magnificent house is in Louisiana.

◁ Bald cypress trees draped in Spanish moss line many rivers, swamps, and bayous in the South. The subtropical flora and fauna give this region a distinctive character, unlike that of any other part of the United States.

△ The South boasts the world-famous Walt Disney World, which includes the Epcot Center. It is located in Orlando, Florida.

# DISTRICT OF COLUMBIA

The District of Columbia is the seat of government of the United States. It covers the same area as the city of Washington, D.C. The Constitution provided that an area of land be set aside for the new nation's capital, and it was authorized by Congress in 1790. George Washington named his choice of a location for the city in 1791. He hired a French architect, Pierre Charles L'Enfant, to design the city. In 1800 the federal government moved the capital from Philadelphia. The District of Columbia was originally made up of small portions of Maryland and Virginia, but the Virginia land was returned to that state in 1846. During the Civil War, Confederate territory began just over the Potomac River, in Virginia.

Because Washington is a district, not a state, its residents used to have fewer rights than other U.S. citizens. For example, until 1961 they did not have the right to vote in presidential elections. Many famous historic buildings are located in the city. The Jefferson Memorial, Washington Monument, and Lincoln Memorial pay tribute to three of America's greatest presidents. Today Washington, D.C. is probably the most important center of government in the world.

HISTORIC CITY
The centerpiece of the nation's capital, Washington, D.C., is its impressive Capitol building on Capitol Hill. The building (above) has undergone many changes since it was first designed by William Thornton in 1793. The federal government is conducted in its House of Representatives and Senate. The Library of Congress is also in Washington. The President of the United States lives in his official residence, the White House, at 1600 Pennsylvania Avenue. Every president except Washington has lived there. Within the Lincoln Memorial, the statue of a seated President Lincoln (right) faces the Washington Monument— a 555-foot (169-m) high obelisk —which can be ascended by elevator. The newest monument was completed in May 2004, and is dedicated to those who died in World War II.

### DISTRICT OF COLUMBIA

**Area**
68 sq. mi.
(177 sq. km)
**Population**
588,292 (2007)
**Principal river**
Potomac
**Highest point**
Tenleytown
410 feet (125m)
**Motto**
*Justitia Omnibus*
(Justice For All)

# THE MIDWESTERN STATES

The Midwest occupies the center of the United States. It adjoins all the other regions, as well as Canada. The land was formed mainly by glaciers retreating after an ice age millions of years ago. These huge masses of ice flattened much of the terrain in the south and left deposits of rich soil. Farming predominates in the region, and the Midwest has long been the "breadbasket" of the United States. It produces most of the country's grain—spring wheat in the north, winter wheat and corn in the center and south. Soybeans are an important crop, especially in Iowa. Only the Badlands and the Black Hills of South Dakota are unsuitable for crops.

The Midwest is also rich in minerals, and iron and steel industries are located here in towns such as Gary, Indiana, and Detroit, Michigan. Chicago is the largest city in the Midwest. It also boasts the nation's tallest building, the Sears Tower. The city stands on the shores of Lake Michigan, one of the five Great Lakes, which form the region's northeastern border.

The Great Lakes alone contain 99 percent of all the fresh water in the country. Several states are dotted with thousands of lesser lakes—Michigan, Minnesota, and Wisconsin have more than 8,000 apiece. The Mississippi–Missouri river system helps shape the geography and economy of the region. Over 12 percent of the total area of North America is drained by the Mississippi and its tributaries. The Midwest accounts for some 20 percent of the total land area, and one fourth of the nation's population. Much of the Midwest was bought from France in 1803 by the U.S. government as part of the Louisiana Purchase.

△ A barrier ridge known as the Wall rises from the prairie in the Badlands National Park, South Dakota. Pioneers feared these fluted escarpments and gave the area the name Badlands. Herds of bison and bighorn sheep now roam the land.

◁ Much of the Midwest is a vast, flat prairie that has been cultivated to produce a large portion of the nation's wheat and other staple crops. These combines are in Kansas, the leading wheat-growing state.

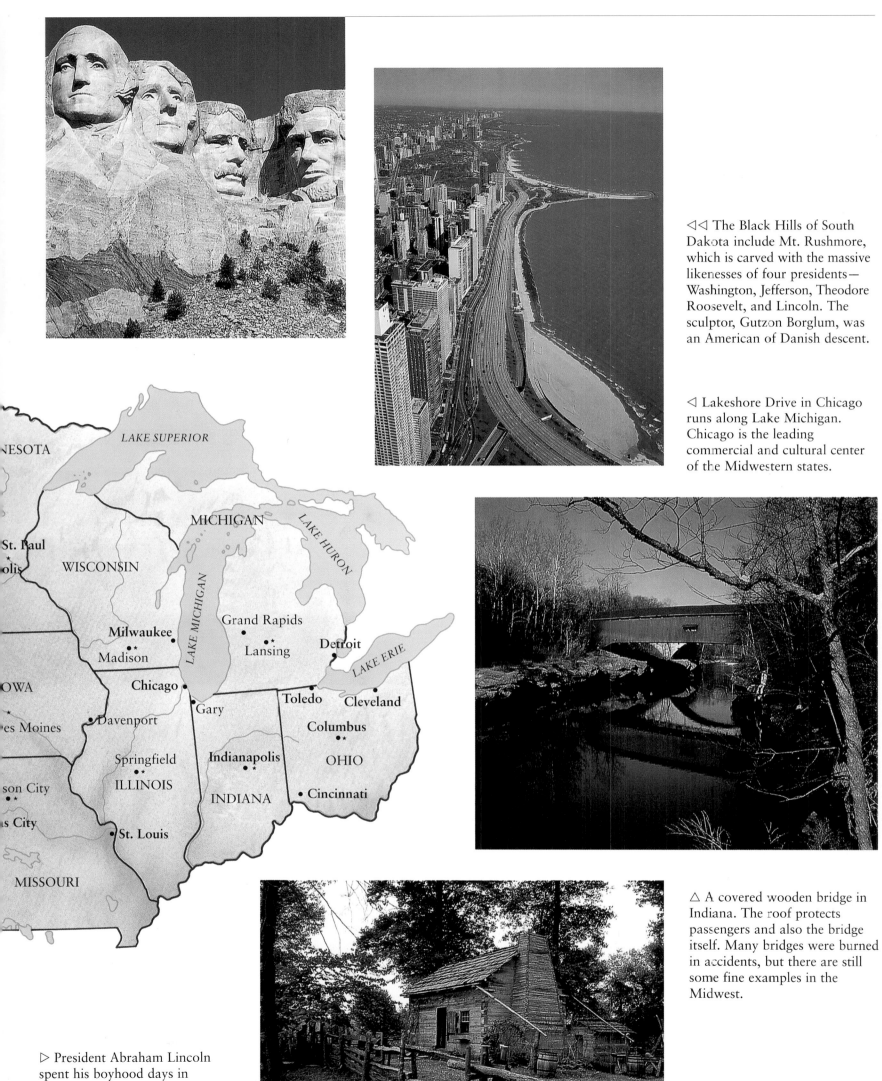

◁◁ The Black Hills of South Dakota include Mt. Rushmore, which is carved with the massive likenesses of four presidents—Washington, Jefferson, Theodore Roosevelt, and Lincoln. The sculptor, Gutzon Borglum, was an American of Danish descent.

◁ Lakeshore Drive in Chicago runs along Lake Michigan. Chicago is the leading commercial and cultural center of the Midwestern states.

△ A covered wooden bridge in Indiana. The roof protects passengers and also the bridge itself. Many bridges were burned in accidents, but there are still some fine examples in the Midwest.

▷ President Abraham Lincoln spent his boyhood days in Indiana, and much of his adult life in Illinois. His early home is located south of Lincoln City, Indiana, at the Lincoln Boyhood National Monument.

# THE SOUTHWESTERN STATES

The Southwestern states of Arizona, New Mexico, Texas, and Oklahoma tell another history of the United States, far removed from the better-known story of the Thirteen Colonies and their struggle for independence. From the 1500s to the mid-1800s this vast territory was dominated by Spaniards and then Mexicans. Spanish influence is still evident here, especially in the architecture and the place-names, such as Santa Fe ("Holy Faith"), the territory's first capital.

Here, too, the culture of Native Americans remains visible. Ancient tribes such as the Anasazi, Zuñi, and Hopi flourished as long as 15,000 years ago. They hunted bison and mammoths and later probably developed the first agriculture on the continent, as well as crafts such as basket weaving and pottery. When the Spanish arrived, they found settled communities, whose village culture they called simply *pueblo* ("town").

The Southwest is a region of vast open plains, mountains, and desert. Its most renowned feature is the Grand Canyon in Arizona, a 277-mile (450-km)-long gorge cut by the Colorado River. With a depth in places of one mile (1.6km), the canyon reveals, in its many layers of beautifully colored rock, the development of the continent over hundreds of millions of years.

Oklahoma was the earliest part of the Southwest to be acquired by the United States, as part of the Louisiana Purchase of 1803. The state of Texas joined the Union in 1845, and most of the remaining southwest territory was acquired as a result of the Mexican War (1846–1848).

| 0 | | 300 kilometers |
| 0 | | 200 miles |

◁ The weaving of traditional blankets provides Navajos with a valuable source of income. Navajos are the largest tribe of Native Americans, with some 160,000 in the Southwest.

▷ Spectacular sandstone monoliths rise up in Arizona's Monument Valley. At sunset they cast long shadows over the great expanse of plateau.

◁ The White Sands National Monument in New Mexico contains great deposits of wind-blown gypsum sand. In strong light, the sands look like a giant snowfield.

◁ The Southwest is a large oil-producing region, with Texas ranked as the second oil-producing state, Oklahoma fifth, and New Mexico sixth. Much of the oil is extracted from the Gulf of Mexico.

△ Cattle herding is still done by cowboys on horseback, as it was in the mid-1800s on many of the vast ranches of the Southwest.

▷ This sculpture by the famous Spanish artist Joan Miró is located in Houston, Texas, the country's fourth-largest city. Houston is well known for its distinctive examples of modern architecture, such as these towering skyscrapers.

# THE ROCKY MOUNTAIN STATES

As their name suggests, the Rocky Mountain states of Colorado, Utah, Wyoming, Montana, Nevada, and Idaho are crossed by this great mountain range—the greatest in North America. The Rockies extend from north to south through the west-central United States. Running along the crest of the mountains is the Continental Divide. Rain falling east of this line forms rivulets and then larger streams and rivers that eventually drain into the Gulf of Mexico or the Great Lakes and on into the Atlantic. Rain falling to the west of it eventually reaches the Pacific.

The Rockies contain several national parks. The best known of these, located mainly in Wyoming, is Yellowstone National Park, which is famous for its many geysers and abundant wildlife. Elk, moose, wolves, and even grizzly bears inhabit this natural wonderland. Grand Teton National Park, also in Wyoming, boasts some of the most spectacular peaks in the Rockies, the highest in the park being Grand Teton itself at 13,770 feet (4,200m).

This region is also rich in minerals—oil, natural gas, copper, gold, silver, lead, zinc, and molybdenum. Farming, too, is important, with thousands of acres devoted to sheep and cattle raising and to crops such as wheat and potatoes.

The largest city of the Rocky Mountain region is Denver, Colorado, which is also one of the highest cities in the United States, with an elevation of exactly one mile (1.6km). Earlier Native American inhabitants of Colorado farmed the high mesas and built their homes in the sandstone cliffs. These amazing cliff dwellings can still be seen today in Mesa Verde National Park.

0          200 kilometers
0          100 miles

Reno
Carson City

NEVADA

Las

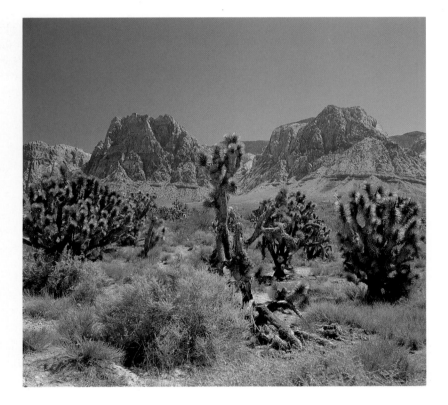

◁ Desert plants and rocky hills in Nevada. This Rocky Mountain state lies almost entirely within a huge desert area that extends into Idaho and Utah.

▷ This snowy scene in Idaho is typical of the Rocky Mountain states in winter. A herd of cattle braves the freezing conditions.

◁ △ An aerial view of farmland contours in Idaho. Rocky Mountain crops include the famous Idaho potato; hay, wheat, barley, oats, and fruit are also grown in the region.

△ As its name implies, Old Faithful geyser in Yellowstone National Park keeps on gushing regularly without fail. It does so at least every half-hour, when it spews out 5–7,000 gallons (19–27,000 liters) of hot water.

△ With so many great rivers flowing through the Rocky Mountains, water sports, especially whitewater rafting, draw thousands of vacationers to these states each year.

◁ Breathtaking mountain scenery is a distinctive feature of this region. There are numerous lakes, waterfalls, hot springs, and glaciers.

# THE PACIFIC COAST STATES

The Pacific Coast states are the nation's last western frontier. They embrace a vast area of the earth's surface—from the three adjoining states of California, Oregon, and Washington, to Alaska in the far northwest and Hawaii, halfway across the Pacific Ocean. Anchorage, on Alaska's south coast, lies 1,500 miles (2,415km) north of Seattle, in Washington, and Honolulu is 2,500 miles (4,025km) from Los Angeles. By contrast, the westernmost point of Alaska is only 50 miles (80km) from Siberia, across the Bering Strait.

Their enormous geographical spread gives the Pacific Coast states the greatest variety of any region, ranging from the frozen tundra of Alaska to the lush, green, volcanic terrain of Hawaii. The mountains, valleys, and coastlines of the three contiguous states offer dramatic landscapes.

In their different ways, the Pacific states are among the richest in natural resources, especially oil and timber. The vast forest of Oregon and Washington supply more of the nation's timber than any other region, and California's fertile valleys produce fruits and vegetables in abundance.

The physical diversity of the Pacific states is matched by their ethnic diversity. As well as Inuit (Eskimos), and native Hawaiians, there are many Asian, white, black, and Hispanic settlers.

◁ The Space Needle dominates the Seattle skyline on Puget Sound. This, the largest city in Washington, is surrounded by snowcapped mountains of the Cascade Range.

△▷ A large walrus colony rests on the shores of the Bering Sea, at the Westernmost tip of Alaska.

◁ Hawaii is not all volcanic craters, tropical forests, and sandy beaches. Inland are important farming areas. These fields either side of the river are growing taro, an edible root vegetable.

△ Mountains and rocks line the shore at Cannon Beach in Oregon. The state's coastline extends 296 miles (476km) along the Pacific Ocean.

◁ Market gardening is an important industry in Washington, Oregon, and California. Apples, citrus fruit, and flowers thrive here. The region also produces most of North America's wine.

▷ San Francisco, on the Pacific coast, spans 14 hills, several of which are linked by a famous cable car system. Attractive wooden houses, cable cars, and these hills give San Francisco a special charm. It is situated on the natural harbor of San Francisco Bay.

# ALABAMA

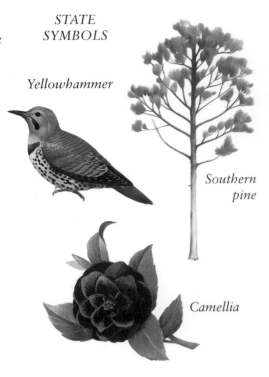

*Yellowhammer*

*Southern pine*

*Camellia*

Located in the heart of the Deep South, Alabama is a state with a rich conflict-filled history. It is a history of wealthy cotton plantations (with the slavery they were based on), bloody civil war, and later social and political change. It was in Montgomery, the state capital, that the Confederate States of America were established on February 4, 1861. The First White House of the Confederacy is located in the city. It was also in Alabama that many of the important events in the civil rights campaigns of the 1950s and 1960s took place.

Alabama has a short strip of coastline on the Gulf of Mexico, dominated by the city of Mobile, at the mouth of the Mobile River. The state's mild climate and rich soil make it an important farming state, growing the traditional southern crops of peanuts, cotton, and pecans. Alabama is also a large lumber producer, and pulp and paper processing are important sources of income. But the state has also taken on 20th-century industries, including electronics and the space industry. Birmingham is the South's leading steel center. Alabama has large reserves of the three most important raw materials used in steel making—coal, limestone, and iron ore. Most of Alabama's farms are located in the fertile, low-lying southern areas. The north is hilly and forested, with many rivers and lakes. Many of the state's rivers have been harnessed to provide power via hydroelectric power stations and dams.

Alabama was occupied by the French and Spanish before the entire region was ceded to England by the French at the end of the French and Indian War in 1763. However, Alabama continued to attract French settlers. The area later became a flourishing cotton-producing center, and some of its fine antebellum houses can still be visited. The Mobile Bay area, including the Gulf Coast State Park, is Alabama's leading tourist area. Its attractions include Bienville Square in Mobile itself, and the Bellingrath Gardens, 20 miles (32km) south of the town. Another of the state's attractions that can be visited is Arlington Home and Gardens in Birmingham. This Greek revival house is the oldest structure in the city and the only mansion to survive the Civil War.

## ALABAMA

**Capital**
Montgomery
**Area**
52,419 sq. mi.
(135,755 sq. km)
**Population**
4,627,851 (2007)
**Largest cities**
Birmingham
(1,108,210)
Mobile (540,258)
**Statehood**
December 14, 1819
Rank: 22nd
**Principal rivers**
Tombigbee, Alabama,
Tennessee
**Highest point**
Cheaha
2,407 feet (734m)
**Motto**
*Audemus Jura Nostra
Defendere* (We Dare
Defend Our Rights)
**Song**
"Alabama"

HELEN KELLER
Writer and scholar, Helen Keller was born in Alabama in 1880. Deaf, blind, and almost without speech from the age of two, Keller (far left) was taught to read, write, and speak by Anne Sullivan (left). Keller "listened" by putting her fingers on the speaker's nose, lips, and throat, and read using braille— a special alphabet for the blind.

TUSKEGEE UNIVERSITY
White Hall at Tuskegee University, the nation's oldest seat of learning for African-Americans. The school was founded by former slave Booker T. Washington in 1881. He served as principal and instructor for 33 years. George Washington Carver, the famous scientific farmer, studied and taught at the college.

## ALABAMA'S SPACE CENTER

The Space and Rocket Center is in Huntsville, in north-central Alabama, and is run by NASA (the National Aeronautics and Space Administration). It is said to be the largest space museum in the world. Visitors can become "astronauts" for a day, experience the sensation of weightlessness on a zero-gravity machine, and guide a spacecraft by computer. Huntsville is also the location of the U.S. Army's Redstone Arsenal and the George C. Marshall Space Flight Center. It was in Huntsville that the booster rockets which carried the Apollo Spacecraft to the moon in 1969 were made.

## BROWN BOMBER

Joe Louis was one of America's greatest boxers. He was born in Alabama in 1914. In the late 1930s he won the world heavyweight title. Over 12 years he successfully defended his title 25 times—20 of these ended in knockouts. Louis, nicknamed the Brown Bomber, retired undefeated, the longest-reigning world heavyweight champion in history. He died in 1981.

## RACCOON

Raccoons live in woods near water. They are found in Alabama and all over the United States. These animals are nighttime hunters and scavengers. They have been hunted for their furs—first by Native Americans and later by white settlers, who used the furs as early currency.

## COTTON WAS KING

Alabama's wealth came originally from cotton until the 1930s, when insect damage from the boll weevil pest, and competition from Texas and California, forced a decline in the cotton industry. Cotton is the soft white hairs, or fibers, that grow on the seeds of the cotton plant.

## MOBILE'S SHIPS

Mobile, on the Gulf of Mexico, is the site of the battleship U.S.S. Alabama Memorial Park. The battleship saw action in World War II and was one of the largest ever built. Next to it is the submarine Drum. Both may be boarded by visitors. Alabama's State Docks in Mobile have made the city an important ocean port. South of the city are beautiful sandy beaches for vacationers. Also in Mobile is Fort Condé–Charlotte, a recreation of an 18th-century French fortress.

# ALASKA

Alaska lives up to its unofficial nickname, "The Last Frontier." It is the most northerly state, a huge peninsula jutting out into the Arctic and Bering seas in the northwest corner of North America. It is completely separated from the continental United States by Canada. Alaska was bought by U.S. Secretary of State William H. Seward from the Russians in 1867. He paid $7.2 million—or about two cents per acre—but the deal was called "Seward's Folly" because the land seemed so desolate.

Almost one third of the state lies in the Arctic Circle, and much of the land is a vast wilderness of frozen tundra, glaciers, ice fields, lakes, spectacular mountains, and forests. It is also by far the largest state—double the land area of the second-largest state, Texas —but has one of the smallest populations. Sixteen percent of the people are native Alaskans—Inuits (Eskimos), Aleuts, and other Native American peoples. Aleuts, who gave the state its name, are related to Inuits but have their own language. Fishing is their main livelihood. Alaska's climate is varied. Some areas have harsh winters, but temperatures do not drop drastically on the Pacific coast because of the warming effect of the Japan Current. Winters are long, and the summer lasts just for June and July, when there are more daylight hours. This is the growing season for the inland valley farmlands, which produce barley, hay, and potatoes. The biggest industries by far are natural oil and gas, followed by tourism and fishing. Oil deposits were first discovered in the late 1950s. The 800-mile (1,300-km) Trans-Alaska Pipeline was built across the frozen wastes to the port of Valdez in the Alaskan Gulf. It was near here that the oil tanker Exxon Valdez spewed the largest oil spill in U.S. history in 1989. The oil slick spread for 45 miles (72km).

## STATE SYMBOLS

*Willow ptarmigan*

*Forget-me-not*

*Sitka spruce*

### SIGNS IN THE SKY
Native American tribes, including Tlinglit and Haida, live in the milder southeast coastal regions. Totem poles are a visible part of their heritage.

### LAND OF NATURAL BEAUTY
The mountains, fjords, and glaciers, such as Mendenhall glacier (below), create a spectacular Arctic scenery that attracts thousands of tourists to Alaska. There are also many active volcanoes in the southeast and southwest of the state. Alaska boasts America's largest national park, Wrangell-St. Elias, covering 13,018 square miles (33,717 sq. km).

| ALASKA | |
|---|---|
| **Capital** | |
| Juneau | |
| **Area** | |
| 663,267 sq. mi. | |
| (1,717,729 sq. km) | |
| **Population** | |
| 683,478 (2007) | |
| **Largest cities** | |
| Anchorage (278,700) | |
| Fairbanks (31,324) | |
| Juneau (30,711) | |
| **Statehood** | |
| January 3, 1959 | |
| Rank: 49th | |
| **Principal rivers** | |
| Yukon | |
| Kuskokwim | |
| **Highest point** | |
| Mt. McKinley 20,320 ft | |
| (6,194m); highest in | |
| North America | |
| **Motto** | |
| North to the Future | |
| **Song** | |
| "Alaska's Flag" | |

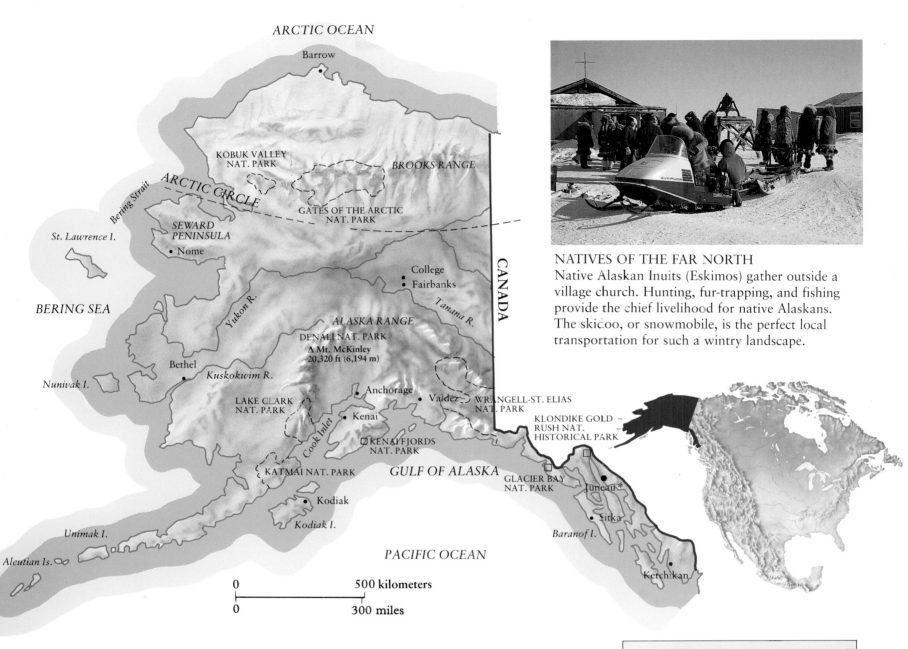

ARCTIC OCEAN
Barrow

KOBUK VALLEY
NAT. PARK
BROOKS RANGE
ARCTIC CIRCLE

*Bering Strait*
GATES OF THE ARCTIC
NAT. PARK
SEWARD
PENINSULA

*St. Lawrence I.*
• Nome

College
• Fairbanks

*Tanana R.*

*BERING SEA*

*Yukon R.*
ALASKA RANGE
DENALI NAT. PARK
Δ Mt. McKinley
20,320 ft (6,194 m)

CANADA

Bethel
*Kuskokwim R.*

*Nunivak I.*
LAKE CLARK
NAT. PARK

• Anchorage
• Valdez
WRANGELL-ST. ELIAS
NAT. PARK

• Kenai
*Cook Inlet*
KENAI FJORDS
NAT. PARK

KLONDIKE GOLD
RUSH NAT.
HISTORICAL PARK

KATMAI NAT. PARK
GULF OF ALASKA
GLACIER BAY
NAT. PARK
Juneau *

*Unimak I.*
• Kodiak
*Kodiak I.*
Sitka
*Baranof I.*

*Aleutian Is.*
PACIFIC OCEAN
Ketchikan

| 0 | 500 kilometers |
| 0 | 300 miles |

BERING SEA
*Aleutian* Is.
PACIFIC OCEAN

## NATIVES OF THE FAR NORTH

Native Alaskan Inuits (Eskimos) gather outside a
village church. Hunting, fur-trapping, and fishing
provide the chief livelihood for native Alaskans.
The skidoo, or snowmobile, is the perfect local
transportation for such a wintry landscape.

## COMMERICIAL CENTER

The business area and port of Anchorage—
Alaska's largest city and business center—
sits on the shores of Cook Inlet, which is
part of the Gulf of Alaska. Huge icebergs
regularly break off from glaciers along the
gulf and are carried out to sea by the
Alaska Current. English explorer Captain
Cook first visited the area in 1778. Oil is
now the chief industry of the city.

## KING OF THE ICE

Swift on land and in the sea, polar bears hunt
seals and fish for food. They grow to about
5 feet (1.5m) in length and inhabit the frozen
lands of Alaska and other Arctic regions.

## ONION DOME

This Russian Orthodox church, with its onion-shaped
dome, is a reminder of the time when the Russians
first settled in the area in the 1700s. Russian
traders were searching for furs, and they
set up a fur trade center on Kodiak
Island in 1784. The territory came
under Russian control, and Alaska's
first capital was founded in New
Archangel (present-day Sitka) in
1804, where other Russian churches
still stand. Sitka is a busy center of
fishing and tourism on the west coast
of Baranof Island.

# ARIZONA

Arizona lies in the heart of the Southwest. It is an area of deserts, mountains, and plateaus, but is best known for being home to America's most famous natural feature —the Grand Canyon. At the canyon's western end lies Lake Mead (part of which is in Nevada and is the reservoir for Hoover Dam), which is one of the largest manmade lakes in the world. Other famous natural landscapes are the Painted Desert, a region of colorful wind-eroded hills, and the Petrified Forest, which has many fossilized trees that have turned to stone over millions of years but have kept their treelike appearance. The southern half of Arizona is part of the Sonoran (or Gila) Desert, which has many varieties of cactuses, such as the giant saguaro and organ pipe, found nowhere else in the world.

Irrigation has made this mainly barren land productive, with cotton and sorghum being among the chief crops. Air-conditioning helps people endure the intense summer heat, and people have been coming to Arizona at a rate that makes it one of the fastest-growing states in the nation. Tourism is also a major industry, as are the manufacture of electronics and mining of molybdenum, gold, and silver. In the days of the Wild West, Tombstone, 30 miles (50km) north of the Mexican border and the neighboring town of Bisbee were made rich by their silver mines.

The Spanish were the first Europeans to settle in the region, where they found Native American civilizations dating back to the 1100s. These Native Americans lived in *pueblos*, structured in a similar way to modern apartment buildings, some four or five stories high. They irrigated and farmed the land. Tucson, the second-largest city, preserves much of its early Spanish flavor. The San Xavier del Bac Mission, near Tucson, was founded in 1692 by Spanish missionaries and is a historic landmark. The Spanish ruled it from the 1500s until 1821, when it became part of the newly independent Mexico. After the Mexican War of 1846–1848 the territory was given to the United States. In the 1860s Arizona was also the site of fierce fighting when Apache and Navajo tribes fought white settlers and the U.S. Army. Today the state has the second-largest Native American population and the largest amount of tribally-owned land.

**SANDRA DAY O'CONNOR**
Born in Texas, Sandra Day O'Connor served her adopted state of Arizona as a prosecutor, senator, and judge. In 1981 she became the first woman appointed to the U.S. Supreme Court.

**AWESOME DESCENT**
The Grand Canyon is etched across the northwestern corner of Arizona. It is 277 miles (450km) long as the river runs, from 4 to 18 miles (6 to 30km) wide, and one mile (1.6km) deep.

STATE SYMBOLS *Cactus wren*

*Paloverde*

*Saguaro cactus*

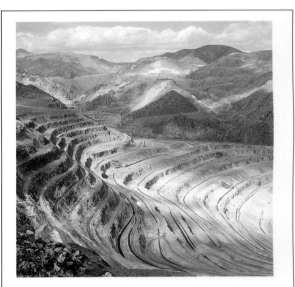

**DIGGING DEEP**
This vast open-pit copper mine reflects Arizona's position as a leading copper producer. At one time the state produced 12 percent of all the world's copper, and Arizona still accounts for 65 percent of total U.S. output. The largest pit in the state is over 1,300 feet (400m) deep. Copper is mined for its long-lasting, pliable, and non-rusting qualities, and it is used in the production of wires and cables, as well as in boilers and radiators. However, such massive open-pit mining of the Earth's surface is a matter of concern to many environmentalists because of the damage it does to the landscape.

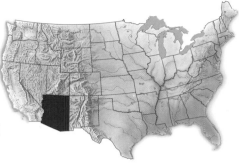

## POISONOUS LIZARD
The Gila monster is aptly named for its looks, its poisonous bite, and its discovery in the Gila Desert. It lives in dry, scrubby areas, hiding in burrows by day and emerging at night to prey on small mammals, such as mice.

### ARIZONA

**Capital**
Phoenix
**Area**
113,998 sq. mi.
(295,232 sq. km)
**Population**
6,338,755 (2007)
**Largest cities**
Phoenix (1,552,259)
Tucson (525,529)
**Statehood**
February 14, 1912
Rank: 48th
**Principal rivers**
Colorado, Gila, Salt
**Highest point**
Humphreys Peak
12,633 feet (3,853m)
**Motto**
*Ditat Deus*
(God Enriches)
**Song**
"Arizona"

## MONTEZUMA CASTLE
This 800-year-old cliff dwelling, in the center of Arizona, was built by Pueblo Indians. The 5-story, 20 room adobe brick structure was named "Montezuma castle" by early Spanish settlers who believed that is was built by Aztec refugees from Mexico —their emperor's name was Montezuma.

## PHOENIX RISING
Named after the mythical bird that was burned and rose again from the ashes, Phoenix, with its many modern skyscrapers, rises out of the arid countryside. The city covers around 350 square miles (990 sq. km) and is located on the Salt River, in the south-central part of the state. It is the state capital and largest city and the fifth-largest city in the United States. Phoenix is a center for electronic and computer industries, as well as for medicine. Most of Arizona's factories are located in and around the city.

25

# ARKANSAS

Located in the south-central part of the United States, Arkansas is essentially a Southern state but also has a western flavor. Its eastern and southern borders touch Mississippi, Tennessee, and Louisiana; on the west it adjoins Texas and Oklahoma. The land is a mixture of Mississippi lowlands, rolling prairie, forests, and mountains. It was first visited by the Spaniards and then explored and settled by the French. As part of the Louisiana Purchase, it was sold to the United States in 1803. The Boston Mountains, part of the Ozarks, lie in northern Arkansas, while the Ouachitas, containing Hot Springs National Park, spread across the west of the state. Many vacationers come to soak in the state's natural spring waters at resorts such as Mammoth Spring and Hot Spring. One of the biggest resort towns, Eureka Springs, is a city cut into the mountainside and has been a resort since 1879. Water temperatures in the springs vary from 95° to 147° F (35° to 63° C). The town has a museum devoted to the temperance (anti-liquor) crusader Carry Nation, famous for smashing up saloons with an ax.

Along with tourism, the state derives much income from its fertile farmland. Food processing is probably the state's most important industry. Before the Civil War, Arkansas was primarily an agricultural state, with many small farms worked by slaves. (During the Civil War Arkansas became a Confederate state.) Today manufacturing is more important than agriculture. The state is rich in minerals and is a leading producer of bauxite—used to make aluminum—most of which is mined near the capital, Little Rock, in the center of the state. Oil is mined near El Dorado, and coal and natural gas are produced near Fort Smith. Copper and molybdenum are also mined.

LITTLE ROCK
The skyline of the state's capital and largest city, Little Rock, which lies on the south side of the Arkansas River. The city was home to William E. Woodruff, who founded the Arkansas Gazette — the oldest newspaper west of the Mississippi. Important civil rights demonstrations took place here in the 1950s and 1960s.

*Pine*

*Mockingbird*

*Apple blossom*

STATE SYMBOLS

DIAMONDS
Over 60,000 diamonds have been found by visitors to Crater of Diamonds State Park—the only active diamond fields open to the public in the United States. The park lies near Murfreesboro, in the southeast of the state, and the Little Missouri River runs through it.

### ARKANSAS

**Capital**
Little Rock
**Area**
53,179 sq. mi.
(137,723 sq. km)
**Population**
2,834,797 (2007)
**Largest cities**
Little Rock (184,500)
Fort Smith (83,461)
Fayetteville
(68,726)
**Statehood**
June 15, 1836
Rank: 25th
**Principal rivers**
Arkansas, Mississippi
**Highest point**
Magazine Mountain
2,753 feet (840m)
**Motto**
*Regnat Populus*
(The People Rule)
**Song**
"Arkansas"

PETIT JEAN STATE PARK
A spectacular, high waterfall dominates the attractive Petit Jean State Park, not far from Little Rock. This river links up with the Arkansas River —itself the longest tributary of the Mississippi-Missouri system. Petit Jean was the nickname of a girl who put on boys' clothing so that she could be with the man she loved in the New World wilderness. The park also has caves and a canyon. The people of Arkansas call their home "the natural state," and the land lives up to its reputation for outdoor enthusiasts. The rivers and streams provide excellent canoeing and white-water rafting, as well as fishing.

## MAYA ANGELOU

Born as Marguerite Johnson in St. Louis, Missouri, in 1928, Maya Angelou grew up to become one of America's most gifted writers. She spent much of her childhood in Stamps, Arkansas, and worked in Egypt and Ghana during the early 1960s. Many of her books recount the experiences of her own life. In *I Know Why the Caged Bird Sings*, the first and best-known of these books, she creates a powerful image of an African-American girl in the South during the Depression. She has also written several volumes of poetry and has worked as an editor, teacher, and movie director.

## RICE FIELDS

Arkansas is the leading producer of rice in the United States. Many rice fields can be found to the east of Little Rock, around Stuttgart. Wild geese and ducks migrating along the Mississippi River stop at the rice fields to rest. Because there are more of these fields than are now needed for rice, some are put to other uses. A few are flooded to form experimental fish farms. Visitors can see the fish farms and also learn about the farming history of the state at the Stuttgart Agricultural Museum. After rice, the most valuable crop is soybeans. Corn is also grown in most of the state, while in the western highlands farmers grow hay, oats, wheat, and fruit. There are also many dairy farms.

## FARMLAND

This is typical farmland in Arkansas, near Fort Smith, close to the state's western border with Oklahoma. Fort Smith itself is a famous historic site, established in 1817 to protect early settlers and covered wagon trains against Native American tribes. In this region crops are grown for about 180 days, but farther south the growing season lasts for about 240 days a year. Fort Smith lies close to the Arkansas River, which cuts the state almost diagonally in half.

## LIZARDS

Reptiles, such as the Eastern fence lizard shown here, thrive in the warm Arkansas wilderness. Lizards are cold-blooded animals, which means they must spend most of the day absorbing warmth from the sun. Arkansas' wooded hills abound with wildlife. Besides lizards there are many kinds of snakes; game birds such as pheasants, quails, and wild turkeys; and mammals such as foxes, deer, and bobcats.

MISSOURI

OZARK PLATEAU
• Eureka Springs
Bull Shoals Lake
• Harrison
• Fayetteville
Dogpatch
□ BLANCHARD SPRINGS CAVERNS
• Mountain View
BOSTON MOUNTAINS
Jonesboro •
St. Francis R.
• Blytheville
55

40
• Fort Smith

△
Magazine Mt.
2,753 ft (840 m)
□ PETIT JEAN STATE PARK
OUACHITA MOUNTAINS
North Little Rock
• Jacksonville
40
• Forrest City
Little Rock ✳
Lake Ouachita
Hot Springs
• Benton
• Stuttgart
• Malvern
HOT SPRINGS NAT. PARK
• Pine Bluff
Arkansas R.
Murfreesboro
30
□
CRATER OF DIAMONDS STATE PARK
• Camden
Mississippi R.

OKLAHOMA

TENNESSEE

MISSISSIPPI

TEXAS
• Texarkana
Red R.
• Magnolia
• El Dorado

0 kilometers    100
0 miles    50

LOUISIANA

# CALIFORNIA

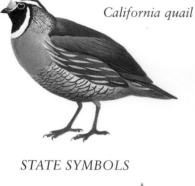

*California quail*

California is the third-largest state. Only Alaska and Texas are larger. It is located on the Pacific coast and stretches 780 miles (1,260km) from the Oregon border in the north to the Mexican border in the south. It has the highest population of any state. Its popular name, the "Golden State," refers to the discovery of gold there in 1848. Today the term could be taken to mean the land of "golden opportunity," for its sunny climate, amazing natural beauty, strong economy, and relaxed lifestyle continue to lure both Americans and immigrants. Los Angeles is the largest city and the second-largest in the nation. It includes the famous district of Hollywood—the center of the movie world. It is also the city of smog— produced by carbon dioxide emissions from the millions of automobiles plying along the 10-lane freeways of the Greater Los Angeles area. To the north lies San Francisco. The city has a famous cable car system originally introduced to relieve horses of the difficult job of dragging streetcars up the city's steep hills. Inland from San Francisco lies the Central Valley, with the San Joaquin River providing a source for well-irrigated citrus fruit groves and farms that produce over 200 other agricultural products. California is also a state of natural wonders. At Yosemite National Park you can see the country's highest waterfall, Yosemite Falls, which drops 2,425 feet (740m) in three cascades. Several parks preserve giant redwood trees, many over 300 feet (90m) tall, and some over 3,000 years old. At Inyo National Forest, the bristlecone pines are believed to be 4,600 years old, which makes them the oldest living things on Earth. In Death Valley, a barren desert, lies the lowest point in North America at 282 feet (86m) below sea level.

**STATE SYMBOLS**

*Golden poppy*

*California redwood*

## CALIFORNIA

**Capital**
Sacramento

**Area**
163,696 sq. mi.
(423,940 sq. km)

**Population**
36,553,215 (2007)

**Largest cities**
Los Angeles
(4,045,873)
San Diego
(1,336,865)

**Statehood**
September 9, 1850
Rank: 31st

**Principal rivers**
Sacramento
Colorado

**Highest point**
Mt. Whitney
14,494 feet (4,418m)

**Motto**
*Eureka*
(I Have Found It)

**Song**
"I Love You,
California"

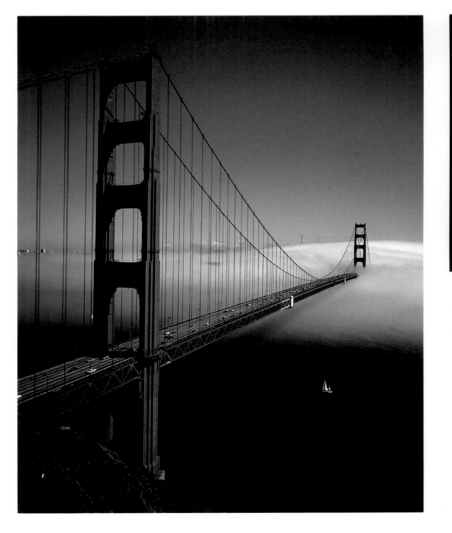

SHROUDED IN CLOUD
The Golden Gate Bridge spans the entrance to San Francisco Bay. It was completed in 1932 and at 4,200 feet (1,280m), is the second-longest suspension bridge in the country. It is often hidden by morning and evening fog rolling in over the hills.

JOHN STENBECK
Nobel Prize-winning novelist John Steinbeck was born in Salinas. Many of his books, including *The Grapes of Wrath* (1940), are realistic and sympathetic portrayals of poor migrant farm workers in the region. Today a museum in Salinas houses Steinbeck's manuscripts and photographs, as well as signed editions of his book.

**POWER IN THE WIND**
Horizontal wind turbines, such as these in Altamont Pass, help produce electricity without polluting the atmosphere.

**WEST COAST WINES**
The vineyards inland from San Francisco in the Napa and Sonoma valleys produce most of the nation's wine. Large vineyards, such as the Mediterranean-style Sterling Vineyard (below) in Calistoga, are open for public tours. There are over 200 wineries in the region, and the grape harvest takes place from September into October. Early Spanish mission padres were the first wine growers.

**PROSPECTING FOR GOLD**
On January 24, 1848, a workman at Sutter's sawmill in northern California found nuggets of gold. News of the find set off a gold rush. Panning for gold (below) in makeshift mining camps was no guarantee of making a fortune for most of the prospectors (gold searchers).

**LIVING ON THE FAULT LINE**
The San Andreas fault (where huge plates of rock deep in the earth's crust meet) runs 270 miles (435km) through west-central California. When the plates move, they cause earthquakes. Despite having buildings strengthened against earthquakes, San Francisco suffered earthquake damage in 1989.

# COLORADO

There is a certain neatness about Colorado. It became a state in 1876—100 years after the signing of the Declaration of Independence—so it is called the "Centennial (100th year) State." It looks like a perfect rectangle on the map, being 387 miles (623km) long from east to west, and 276 miles (444km) long from north to south.

Colorado is one of the Rocky Mountain states. More than half of the state is rugged and mountainous, with over 1,000 peaks above 10,000 feet (3,000m) high. Eastern Colorado is flatter and marks the western edge of the Great Plains. Most of Colorado's population live here, especially in and around Denver, the capital of the state and also the largest city of the

Great Plains. But even Denver lies one mile (1.6km) above sea level, and the state has the highest average elevation in the nation. The major river in the western United States, the Colorado, has its source in the state, as does the Rio Grande. Towering mountains, mighty rivers, and sprawling plains make Colorado one of the most dramatically beautiful states. Tourism is a major industry, with skiers coming to Vail and Aspen in the winter. Another source of income is Colorado's varied mineral wealth—gold, silver, copper, zinc, manganese, molybedenum, coal, lead, and uranium.

Eastern Colorado formed part of the Louisiana Purchase in 1803. Much of the rest of the state comes from territory that was handed over by Mexico after the Mexican War in 1848.

*Lark bunting*

STATE SYMBOLS

*Blue spruce*

*Rocky Mountain colombine*

## ANCIENT CLIFF PALACE
Set in the recessed rock, these cliff dwellings were built centuries ago by Native Americans who farmed the local region. This ancient cliff-dwelling civilization flourished from around 500 B.C. to A.D. 1300. These cliff palaces are preserved in the Mesa Verde National Park.

## THE AGRICULTURAL STATE
About half of Colorado is grazing land, and cattle and sheep ranching are primary industries. Cattle raising is the largest source of farm income, and there is plenty of diary farming. In this picture cattle and sheep graze beneath the snow-covered peaks of the Rocky Mountains. Corn, wheat, hay, and sugar beets are the main crops grown in the state.

## COLORADO POTATO BEETLE
Colorado potato beetles, or potato bugs as they are also called, do terrible damage to potato crops. In their natural Rocky Mountain home, they live on a wild plant that is a member of the potato family. When early settlers planted potatoes in Colorado, the bettles took to the new crop instead.

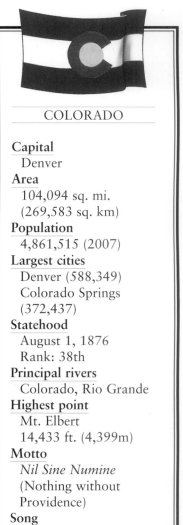

### COLORADO

**Capital**
Denver
**Area**
104,094 sq. mi.
(269,583 sq. km)
**Population**
4,861,515 (2007)
**Largest cities**
Denver (588,349)
Colorado Springs
(372,437)
**Statehood**
August 1, 1876
Rank: 38th
**Principal rivers**
Colorado, Rio Grande
**Highest point**
Mt. Elbert
14,433 ft. (4,399m)
**Motto**
*Nil Sine Numine*
(Nothing without
Providence)
**Song**
"Where the
Columbines Grow"

## MAROON BELL MOUNTAINS

Blue spruce and delicate blue columbines, the state tree and flower, grow in abundance in this area of the Rocky Mountains toward the center of Colorado. Nearby is one of the world's most famous ski resorts, Aspen. Aspen also has a well-known environmental center. Rocky Mountain National Park, in northern Colorado, has more than 100 peaks over 10,000 feet (3,000m) high.

## DENVER SKYLINE

Colorado's capital, Denver, is exactly 5,280 feet (1,600m) above sea level, so it is known as the Mile-High City. It is the industrial, commercial, and transportation center of the Rocky Mountain region, and its size and importance are reflected by its modern skyscrapers. Denver is also the home of the U.S. Mint, where millions of coins are produced, or minted, each year. There are only two other federal mints in the country.

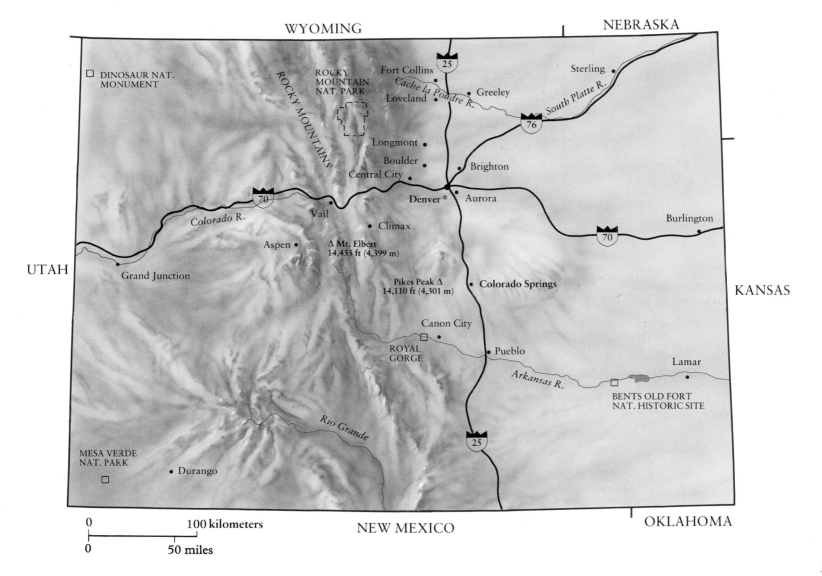

# CONNECTICUT

Located on the northeastern seaboard, with 250 miles (403km) of Atlantic coastline, Connecticut is the southernmost of the New England states. It is also the third-smallest in size and stretches only 95 miles (153km) from east to west, and 60 miles (97km) north to south. Two areas of mainly wooded hilly country border a central river valley region. It is a historic state, and its state nickname, the "Constitution State," refers to its system of government, based on what is believed to be the first written constitution in America dating back to the 1600s. Connecticut also has the country's oldest continuously published newspaper, The Hartford Courant, the country's first public school, and the first warship, the Oliver Cromwell. In 1707 the nation's first copper mine was opened in East Granby. It was later converted by the British into a prison to house enemies of colonial rule.

Connecticut was originally the home of the Pequot tribe of Native Americans. They were defeated by British settlers from Massachusetts in 1637, and the area was one of the first in the United State to be settled by Europeans. The state played an important part in the American Revolution and in the drawing up of the U.S. Constitution. Delegates proposed the Connecticut Compromise, by which all states would have equal representation in the Senate, but representation would be based on population in the House of Representatives—a basis for government that survives today.

## STATE CAPITOL
Connecticut's elegant, gold-domed capitol building in Hartford was built in 1879. It contains mementos of the Revolutionary War and is the meeting place of the state legislature. Across the street in the State Library building is housed the table upon which President Abraham Lincoln signed the Emancipation Proclamation, which freed the slaves of the Confederate states.

### STATE SYMBOLS

*White oak*

*American robin*

*Mountain laurel*

## THE AGE OF SAIL
The reconstructed early 19th-century whaling seaport of Mystic lies on the Mystic River, by Long Island Sound. Connecticut's long shoreline once made it the leading whaling state, as well as supporting a thriving oyster- and lobster-fishing industry. In the 1800s New England's whaling fleets set sail from ports such as Mystic. Restored sea captains' houses, taverns, shops, and galleries with seafaring treasures line the harbor front, and there are old steamboats and whaling ships to explore—one of which hunted whales for 80 years.

## CLASSIC REVOLVER
The famous Colt revolvers that "won the West" were invented and manufactured in Hartford. There are many early rifles and revolvers on view in the city's museums. It was the gun manufacturer Samuel Colt who pioneered the use of interchangeable parts that made mass-production of guns possible.

**CONNECTICUT**

**Capital**
Hartford

**Area**
5,543 sq. mi. (14,355 sq. km)

**Population**
3,502,309 (2007)

**Largest cities**
Bridgeport (137,912)
Hartford (124,512)

**Statehood**
January 9, 1788
Rank: 5th

**Principal rivers**
Connecticut, Housatonic

**Highest point**
Mt. Frissill, 2,380 ft. (726m)

**Motto**
*Qui Transtulit Sustinet*
(He Who Transplanted
Still Sustains)

**Song**
"Yankee Doodle"

### CORN FARM

Although very industrialized, Connecticut is known for its rolling countryside dotted with small farms, such as this one with its field of corn. Corn is the chief vegetable grown in the state. Most of Connecticut's income, however, comes from manufacturing and commerce.

### HARRIET BEECHER STOWE

This Connecticut-born author wrote one of the most famous anti-slavery novels, *Uncle Tom's Cabin*. When President Abraham Lincoln met Harriet Beecher Stowe during the Civil War, he said, "So you're the little lady who wrote the book that caused this great war."

### YALE UNIVERSITY

One of the nation's great seats of learning, Yale University, is situated in New Haven, Connecticut, near Long Island Sound. It was founded in 1701 and is the third-oldest college in the United States. Until 1969 it was a male-only college. It was named after a wealthy English merchant, Elihu Yale, who made his money from trade in the East Indies. He contributed rare books and goods from the East Indies, which were sold to raise the money to build the new college. Its library holds six million books and is one of the largest in the country. The university also has an art gallery and a museum of natural history.

# DELAWARE

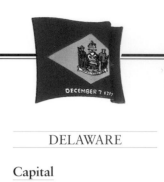

Delaware is nicknamed the "First State" because it was the first to approve the new U.S. Constitution on December 7, 1787. Apart from being the oldest state of the Union, it is also the second-smallest, after Rhode Island. It measures only 96 miles (155km) from north to south and 35 miles (56km) from east to west. Delaware lies on the Atlantic coast between Maryland, Pennsylvania, and New Jersey. The historic Mason-Dixon Line, which fixed the boundary between Maryland and Pennsylvania, also marks Delaware's north-south border with Maryland. Englishman Samuel Argall of the Virginia colony sailed up the present Delaware Bay and named it after Thomas De La Warr, governor of Virginia. In 1638 the New Sweden Company sent out an expedition headed by Peter Minuit to settle the area as New Sweden. Minuit founded Fort Christina, near the present city of Wilmington, the largest in the state. Wilmington still has close ties with Sweden. In 1655 the Dutch conquered New Sweden, but in 1664 the English captured it from the Dutch, renaming it New York. Delaware was formed from part of this colony. The capital, Dover, was founded in 1717. It is one of the oldest and smallest state capitals.

Delaware's industry and economy are closely tied to one family—the Du Ponts. Éleuthère Irénée Du Pont started a firm to make gunpowder in 1802. The Du Pont company no longer makes gunpowder, but it is a world-leading manufacturer of chemicals (Wilmington has been called the chemical capital of the world), plastics, synthetic fibers, dyes, and paints. Delaware is an important business center, with favorable company laws that have attracted hundreds of thousands of U.S. companies to set up corporations in the state—even though they may conduct most of their business elsewhere. Fishing and tourism also aid the state's economy.

Delaware has several wildlife reserves, including the Bombay Hook Wildlife Refuge, a haven for water birds, and the Great Cypress Swamp, the northernmost natural stand of cypress tress in the country.

| DELAWARE |
| --- |
| **Capital** |
| Dover |
| **Area** |
| 2,489 sq. mi. |
| (6,446 sq. km) |
| **Population** |
| 864,764 (2007) |
| **Largest cities** |
| Wilmington (72,826) |
| Dover (34,735) |
| **Statehood** |
| December 7, 1787 |
| Rank: 1st |
| **Principal rivers** |
| Delaware |
| Mispillion |
| Nanticoke |
| **Highest point** |
| Centerville |
| 442 feet (135m) |
| **Motto** |
| Liberty and |
| Independence |
| **Song** |
| "Our Delaware" |

## FISHING FOR A LIVING

Commercial fishing brings in over $4 million a year to Delaware's economy. Menhaden is the chief catch. A type of herring, it provides oil, fish meal, and fertilizers. Freshwater fishing is a popular pastime. Fishermen find bass, carp, catfish, eels, pike, trout, and white perch in Delaware's lakes, ponds, and streams.

*American eel*

*Pike*

*Largemouth bass*

## FARMLAND

Delaware has good soil for farming. In the north of the state are most of the dairy farms and grain farms, such as this one, pictured in winter. Poultry, fruit, and vegetable farming are concentrated in the central and southern areas. The main crops are soybeans, corn, potatotes, and mushrooms. Vegetable and fruit crops include beans, squash, spinach, tomatoes, pumpkins, and melons.

*STATE SYMBOLS*

*American holly*

*Peach blossom*

*Blue hen chicken*

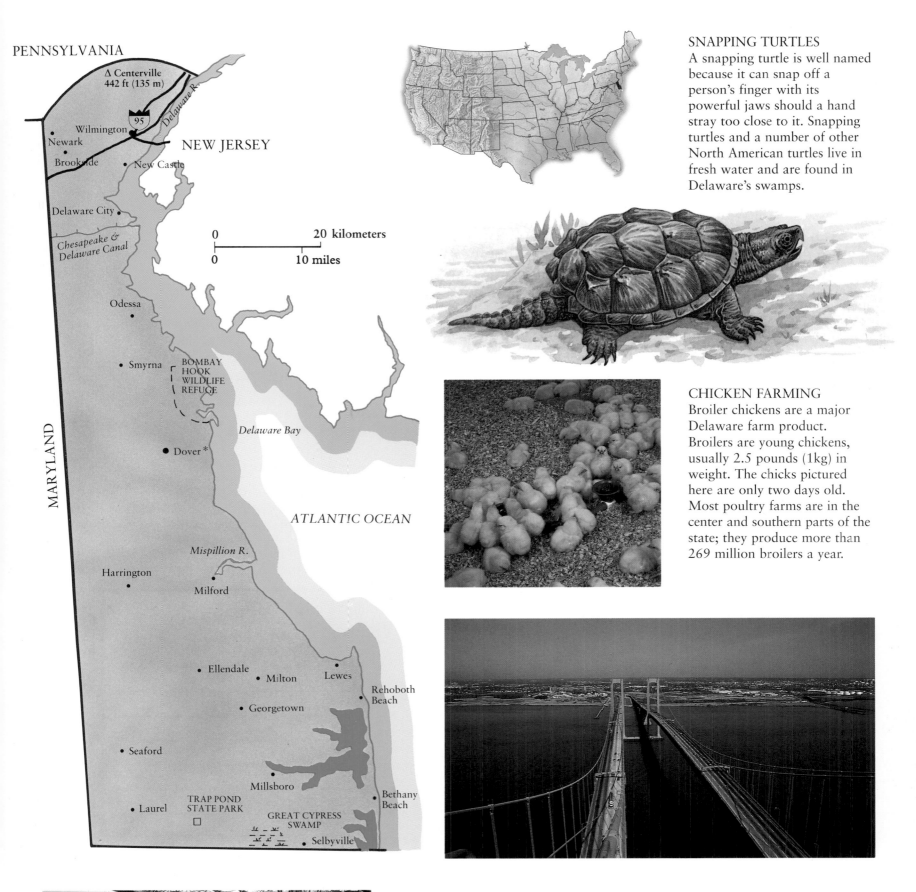

PENNSYLVANIA

Δ Centerville
442 ft (135 m)

95

Delaware R.

Wilmington

Newark

Brookside

New Castle

NEW JERSEY

Delaware City

Chesapeake &
Delaware Canal

0          20 kilometers
0          10 miles

Odessa

MARYLAND

Smyrna

BOMBAY
HOOK
WILDLIFE
REFUGE

Delaware Bay

Dover *

ATLANTIC OCEAN

Mispillion R.

Harrington

Milford

Ellendale
Milton        Lewes

Rehoboth
Beach

Georgetown

Seaford

Millsboro

Bethany
Beach

Laurel

TRAP POND
STATE PARK

GREAT CYPRESS
SWAMP

Selbyville

## SNAPPING TURTLES

A snapping turtle is well named because it can snap off a person's finger with its powerful jaws should a hand stray too close to it. Snapping turtles and a number of other North American turtles live in fresh water and are found in Delaware's swamps.

## CHICKEN FARMING

Broiler chickens are a major Delaware farm product. Broilers are young chickens, usually 2.5 pounds (1kg) in weight. The chicks pictured here are only two days old. Most poultry farms are in the center and southern parts of the state; they produce more than 269 million broilers a year.

## "THE DU PONT STATE"

The Hagley Museum is located on the original site of the Du Pont gunpowder works in Wilmington. The museum complex features restored mills, a water wheel with water turbine, and other machines of the early-1800s. The colonial-style house seen here was built by E. I. Du Pont in 1803. He started the family business that is now the single major corporation in the state. The museum houses antiques from five generations of the family. There are other Du Pont family mansions in Delaware, with beautiful gardens and lavish antiques.

## MEMORIAL BRIDGE

A twin road bridge that spans the Delaware River, the Delaware Memorial Bridge joins Delaware with New Jersey south of Wilmington. It is the largest twin-span suspension bridge in the world. Over 60,000 vehicles cross the bridge each day. The Delaware River flows from New York State south through New Jersey and Pennsylvania and then to Delaware. It is 280 miles (450km) long.

# FLORIDA

Florida is the southernmost state on the U.S. mainland and is aptly named the "Sunshine State"—it rarely freezes as far south as Miami. The state's ideal warm climate has made it one of the most popular retirement and vacation spots for people from other states and from overseas. Three out of four residents originally come from outside the state, an influx which has led to rapid urbanization. Florida has more senior citizens than any other state.

Florida's sunshine has made it the number one orange- and grapefruit-growing state. It is also the leading honey producer and exports avocados, pomegranates, mangoes, and other exotic fruits. Orange farming began with Spanish settlers in 1536 around St. Augustine—the first permanent European settlement in North America. St. Augustine has a layout that is typical of a 16th-century Spanish city. The center of the state, around Orlando, is now the main area for cultivation. This is also the site for the state's major beef and dairy cattle industry. Orlando is home to the famous Walt Disney World, including the Epcot Center and Animal Kingdom.

Florida has no mountains or high hills. Its low-lying terrain, combined with high humidity and heavy bursts of rainfall, has created many swamps and lakes. The biggest lake is Lake Okeechobee in the southeast, which covers about 700 square miles (1,800 sq. km). It is the largest lake in the southern United States. Jacksonville, in the northeast corner, is the state's largest city and the largest in land area in the contiguous United States. The St. Johns River, which runs through the city, is one of the few rivers in the United States that flows from south to north. South of Miami lies the Everglades, which is the largest subtropical wilderness in the mainland United States. It contains the only U.S. mangrove swamps.

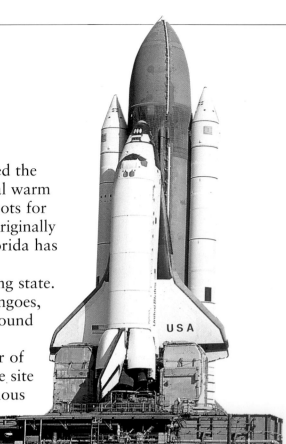

**SPACE SHUTTLE**
Visitors to the John F. Kennedy Space Center, Cape Canaveral, may be lucky enough to witness the launch of a space shuttle. It was from here that the first U.S. manned flight left in 1961, as did the lunar-landing flight on July 16, 1969 carrying Neil Armstrong, the first man on the Moon.

**SEA SIRENS**
Manatees are mammals, so they must come to the surface to breathe. There are about 1,000 manatees, or seacows, surviving in Florida's waters, where they are a protected species. They can live for up to 50 years.

**ISLAND CHAIN**
Off the tip of Florida are the Florida Keys. These are a chain of islands and reefs linked by a central causeway, which form an arc into the Gulf of Mexico. Key West, the southernmost island, provided a working place for American writers Tennessee Williams, John Dos Passos, and Ernest Hemingway. The islands and keys lie just over 90 miles (140km) from Cuba.

*STATE SYMBOLS*

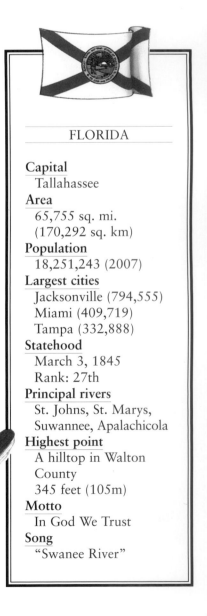

*Palmetto palm*

*Orange blossom*

*Mockingbird*

### FLORIDA

**Capital**
Tallahassee
**Area**
65,755 sq. mi.
(170,292 sq. km)
**Population**
18,251,243 (2007)
**Largest cities**
Jacksonville (794,555)
Miami (409,719)
Tampa (332,888)
**Statehood**
March 3, 1845
Rank: 27th
**Principal rivers**
St. Johns, St. Marys,
Suwannee, Apalachicola
**Highest point**
A hilltop in Walton
County
345 feet (105m)
**Motto**
In God We Trust
**Song**
"Swanee River"

## HOTEL CHAIN
Some seven million tourists come annually to the slim barrier island of Miami Beach to visit its hundreds of hotels and one long beach—seen here separated from mainland Miami by Biscayne Bay. Once almost completely eroded, a 10-mile (16-km) stretch of the Oceanside beach has been restored with breakwaters and reefs.

## GATORS GALORE!
Alligators thrive in the wild subtropical swamplands of Florida. They can grow up to 19 feet (5.8m) long. They eat fish, frogs, snakes, and even small deer. There are many alligator farms and zoos in the state, and alligators are a protected species.

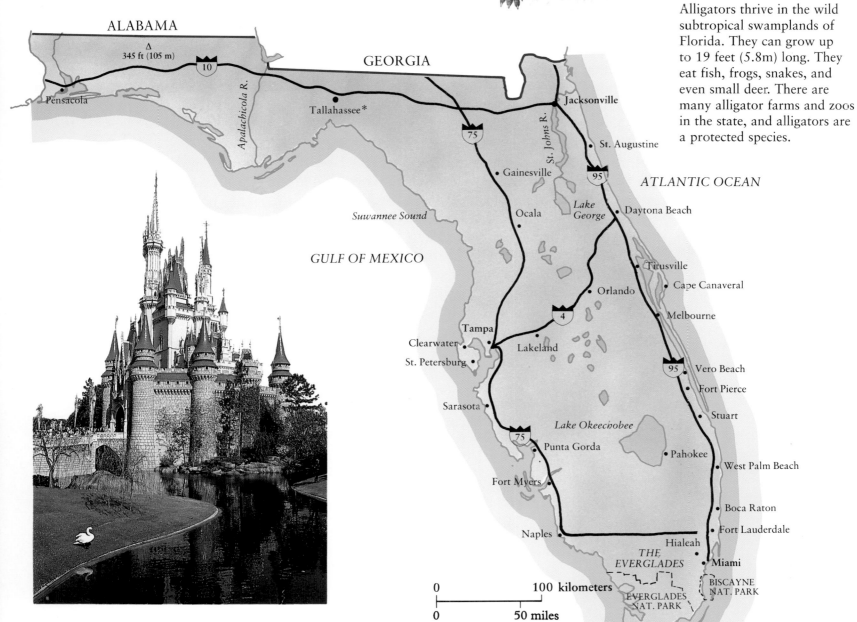

## MAGICAL KINGDOM
Walt Disney World now includes four attractions: the Magic Kingdom, the Epcot Center, Disney-MGM Studios, and Animal Kingdom. Both are located near Orlando in central Florida. One of the most famous symbols of Walt Disney World is Cinderella's Castle (above).

# GEORGIA

Located in the southeast corner of the country to the north of Florida, Georgia is the largest state east of the Mississippi River —almost the same size as the New England states combined. This is one reason for its nickname, "Empire State of the South"— the other being its prosperity. Atlanta, the capital, is the commercial and financial hub of the Southeast.

Georgia's wealth derives chiefly from farming—especially soybeans, peanuts, tobacco, corn, and wheat. Even today many Georgians live on farms and around small towns. Rural Georgia still resembles the old pre-Civil War South, with its economy based on staple crops, though cotton is no longer the major crop. The peaches for which Georgia is famous are still grown but mainly along its Atlantic coast.

The Blue Ridge Mountains rise in northeastern Georgia, a region of dense pine forests. Besides providing valuable timber, this region attracts hunters, fishermen, and tourists. West of these mountains lies the fertile Appalachian Valley, and to the south is the Piedmont, a plateau where Atlanta is situated, together with many large farms. The plateau drops to the coastal plain—the largest part of the state, and which includes Okefenokee Swamp. The swamp is now a wildlife refuge.

Georgia was founded in 1733 by James Oglethorpe, who named the colony in honor of King George II of England. Before his arrival, Creek and Cherokee Indians lived in the area, and Spanish and French explorers had arrived in the 1500s. The state has seen both Revolutionary War and Civil War battles and was badly damaged during the Civil War. In the 1960s Georgia was greatly involved in the civil rights movement, led by Martin Luther King, Jr.

*Live oak*

*Cherokee rose*

SOLDIERS SET IN STONE
Confederate war heroes Jefferson Davis, Robert E. Lee, and Stonewall Jackson are carved into the light-gray granite of Stone Mountain near Atlanta. They stand some 90 feet (27m) high by 190 feet (58m) wide. Stone Mountain itself is the largest smooth-sided rock dome in North America, and measures 2 miles (3.2km) long by 1 mile (1.6km) wide.

*Brown thrasher*

STATE SYMBOLS

ATLANTA
Once called Terminus, because it stood at the southern end, or terminus, of a major rail network, Atlanta remains the transportation center of the state. Its airport is the busiest in the nation. It is also the state capital, largest city, and center of Georgia's thriving textile industry. The skyscrapers signal that this is a modern, industrial city, yet it has not forgotten its Southern heritage.

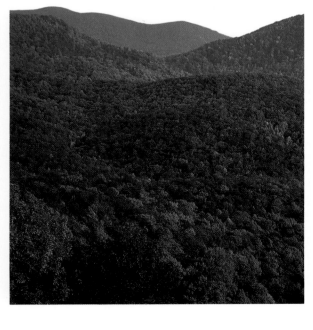

A TREE-LINED STATE
The Blue Ridge Mountains in northeast Georgia are covered with pine trees. Forests once extended over the whole state, and even today 24.4 million acres of Georgia is covered with trees. The state ranks first in the growth of timber. Pine trees yield pulpwood, which is used to produce paper.

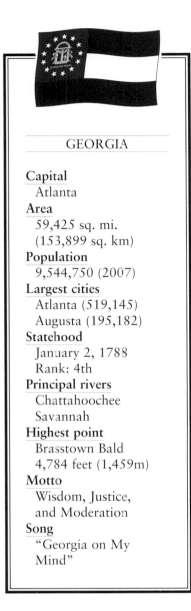

## GEORGIA

**Capital**
Atlanta
**Area**
59,425 sq. mi.
(153,899 sq. km)
**Population**
9,544,750 (2007)
**Largest cities**
Atlanta (519,145)
Augusta (195,182)
**Statehood**
January 2, 1788
Rank: 4th
**Principal rivers**
Chattahoochee
Savannah
**Highest point**
Brasstown Bald
4,784 feet (1,459m)
**Motto**
Wisdom, Justice,
and Moderation
**Song**
"Georgia on My
Mind"

### VAST SWAMP
Spanish moss hangs from the semi-submerged trees in Okefenokee Swamp, at the southern end of Georgia. The swamp is the largest freshwater swamp in the United States and contains the Okefenokee National Wildlife Refuge. Alligators, bears, raccoons, and many birds are among the animals protected there. The swamp was once part of the Atlantic Ocean, but it is now around 100 feet (30m) above sea level.

### MARTIN LUTHER KING, JR.
The Reverend Martin Luther King, Jr., born in Atlanta in 1929, was the nation's most famous African-American. He aimed to promote political, social, educational, and economic rights for African-Americans through non-violent demonstrations. Martin Luther King Jr. was assassinated in 1968, four years after receiving the Nobel Prize for Peace.

### NOT A NUT, BUT A PEA
Georgia is the largest peanut-growing state, and the United States is one of the world's leading producers of this vegetable. Peanuts are eaten not only as a snack but also in foods such as peanut butter and peanut brittle. Peanuts can be crushed for oil as well as for use in many products, including shampoo and even paint. They are also used to feed livestock.

# HAWAII

The youngest and most tropical state of the United States, Hawaii is the only one that does not lie on the North American mainland. It is a chain of 132 volcanic islands in the Pacific Ocean—the only state to be made up entirely of islands—lying about 2,400 miles (3,900km) southwest of San Francisco. This also makes it the most southerly state, and Hilo, on the island of Hawaii, is the southernmost city in the United States.

The islands are the peaks of huge underwater volcanoes. After Hawaii, the largest island, the other major islands in order of size are Maui, Oahu, Kauai, Molokai, Lanai, Niihau, and Kahoolawe. Almost 80 percent of the people live on Oahu, many of them in and around Honolulu, the state's capital.

Tourism is the main source of prosperity, and millions of Americans flock to Hawaii to enjoy the warm climate, the coral reefs, sandy beaches, surfing waves, lush, tropical mountain scenery, and relaxed, friendly lifestyle. The word *Aloha*, from which the state gets its nickname, means "love" in the Hawaiian language (whose alphabet has only 12 letters). The weather is not always sunny; in fact Mt. Waialeale, on Kauai, has the highest annual rainfall in the United States. Such a wet environment is ideal for the cultivation of subtropical crops such as sugar cane and pineapples. The original Hawaiians were Polynesians, who sailed to the islands over 2,000 years ago in great canoes. Today they make up only one percent of the population. Many residents have come from Japan, the Philippines, China, and other parts of Asia. Captain James Cook was probably the first European to reach Hawaii in 1778. In the 1820s many missionaries from the United States began to settle there. Hawaii became a U.S. territory in 1900.

*Nene (Hawaiian goose)*  *Hibiscus*

STATE SYMBOLS  *Kukui (Candlenut)*

BEACH OF DREAMS
Waikiki Beach, near Honolulu on Oahu, is one of the most popular tourist attractions in the United States. It has become somewhat spoiled by its own popularity, with over-development of hotels and crowded beaches. With the hottest and coolest days of the year differing in temperature by as little as 10°F (5°C), the beaches of Hawaii provide recreation all year round. The famous Diamond Head promontory in the background is an extinct volcanic crater. Near the beach are the yacht harbor and Kapiolani Park.

DECEMBER 7, 1941
"A date which will live in infamy," said President Franklin D. Roosevelt, referring to the Japanese aerial attack on Pearl Harbor, which caused heavy losses and crippled the U.S. fleet during World War II. However, many damaged warships were salvaged, and the base was quickly repaired to become the headquarters of the U.S. war in the Pacific. A memorial, built over the partly-submerged battleship Arizona, which sank with more than 1,000 sailors, honors the dead. Pearl Harbor was an important base in both the Korean and Vietnam wars.

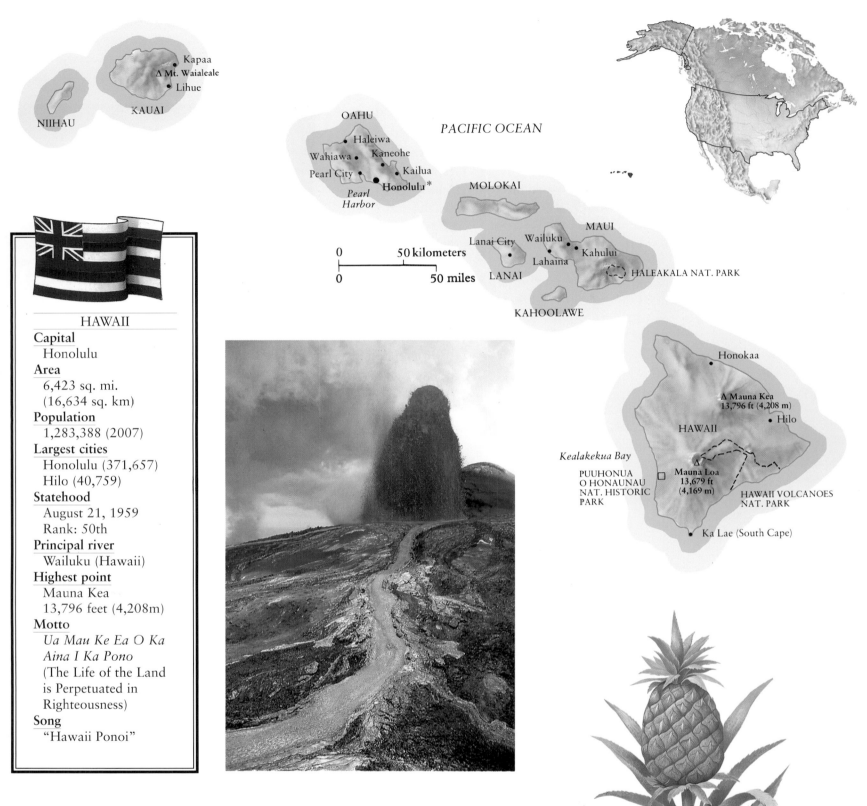

## HAWAII

**Capital**
Honolulu

**Area**
6,423 sq. mi.
(16,634 sq. km)

**Population**
1,283,388 (2007)

**Largest cities**
Honolulu (371,657)
Hilo (40,759)

**Statehood**
August 21, 1959
Rank: 50th

**Principal river**
Wailuku (Hawaii)

**Highest point**
Mauna Kea
13,796 feet (4,208m)

**Motto**
*Ua Mau Ke Ea O Ka
Aina I Ka Pono*
(The Life of the Land
is Perpetuated in
Righteousness)

**Song**
"Hawaii Ponoi"

### THE FIRST HAWAIIANS
Polynesian children pose for the camera. They are direct descendants of the first settlers, who sailed to Hawaii from islands in the western Pacific between A.D. 300 and 750. The first schools were founded by missionaries in the 1840s.

### LAVA FLOW
The Hawaiian Islands were formed by volcanoes over millions of years. They rise up from the Pacific Ocean floor as deep as 18,000 feet (5,500m). Hawaii has the largest active and inactive volcanoes in the world. Haleakala, on Maui, is the largest inactive volcano— its crater measures 33 square miles (85 sq. km). It rises just over 10,000 feet (3,000m), and the crater's interior is home to the rare silversword plant. Massive Mauna Loa, on Hawaii, is one of the most active volcanoes and threatens nearby human settlements.

### PRICKLY FRUIT
Pineapples are an important crop in Hawaii. Although not native to the islands, they thrive there, and the state is the world's biggest exporter of the fruit. Pineapple plantations were started in the 1800s, and by the end of the century were making their owners wealthy. High fields are maintained by the use of irrigation and machinery for both planting and harvesting. Most canned pineapple used in the United States comes from Hawaii. Sugar cane and macadamia nuts are also important exports.

41

# IDAHO

Nicknamed the "Gem of the Mountains" to describe its stunning scenic beauty as well as its natural wealth in gemstones and precious metals, Idaho is a large northwestern state. When it was made a territory in 1863, it was even larger than Texas, but Montana and Wyoming were later taken away from the territory, leaving the state of Idaho with its current rank as the 13th-largest state in the Union.

Much of Idaho is mountainous: the Bitterroot Range includes the Salmon River Mountains, which rise up in the central part of the state, and the Clearwater Mountains, which extend north to Canada. This latter range forms part of the Rocky Mountains. Idaho has a curious, somewhat houselike shape, with a "chimney" abutting the Canadian border. Its low population, around 1.5 million, gives it a density of only 16 people to every square mile. Over 70 percent of the people live within 30 miles (50km) of the Snake River in the south of the state. This is also where Idaho's farmlands are located, and the irrigated fields of volcanic soil along the river are the planting grounds not only for the famous Idaho potatoes, but also for wheat, sugar beets, and barley. Idaho grows more potatoes—and raises more commercial trout—than any other state. Most crops are transported through the capital and largest city, Boise, which lies on a branch of the Snake River. Sheep and cattle raising are also important in this area. Tourism, skiing, and other outdoor activities, such as hunting and trekking, provide a growing income. The first white settlers in what were Nez Percé and Shoshone Native American lands were fur traders and Jesuit missionaries, who arrived in the 1830s. In the 1860s Mormons set up Idaho's first permanent settlement. A gold rush occurred at the same time, and more settlers arrived, forcing the Native Americans to give up their land.

### BOOM AND BUST
Silver City Ghost Town is a relic of Idaho's mining boom from the 1860s. Although it also had a gold rush, Idaho became the leading silver producer in the United States, until the falling price of silver forced many mines to close. There are many old gold- and silver-mining ghost towns, such as Centerville, Placeville, and Pioneerville.

*Mountain bluebird*

STATE SYMBOLS

*Syringa*

*Western white pine*

### LEWIS AND CLARK EXPEDITION
The famous American explorers Meriwether Lewis and William Clark were the first whites known to pass through this region, en route from St. Louis, Missouri, to the Pacific Ocean in 1805. They traveled via the Bitterroot Range through a pass in what is now Montana. The two men were greatly helped by local Native Americans, particularly the Nez Percé and the Shoshone. A Shoshone woman, Sacagawea, gave messages of peace to the local tribes Lewis and Clark met. They also exchanged gifts as a gesture of goodwill. The explorers collected plant and mineral specimens on their 4,000-mile (6,400-km) journey.

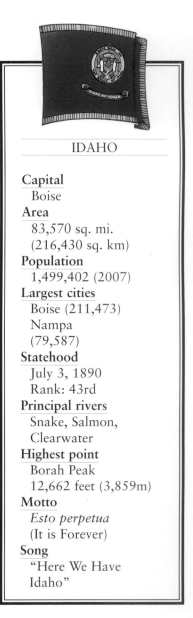

### IDAHO

**Capital**
Boise
**Area**
83,570 sq. mi.
(216,430 sq. km)
**Population**
1,499,402 (2007)
**Largest cities**
Boise (211,473)
Nampa
(79,587)
**Statehood**
July 3, 1890
Rank: 43rd
**Principal rivers**
Snake, Salmon,
Clearwater
**Highest point**
Borah Peak
12,662 feet (3,859m)
**Motto**
*Esto perpetua*
(It is Forever)
**Song**
"Here We Have
Idaho"

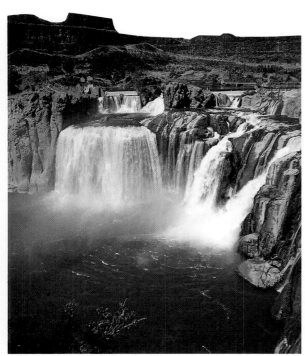

## A STATE OF MANY FALLS
Rivers, particularly the Snake River, are a prominent feature of Idaho's landscape. The Snake River rushes westward, its journey punctuated by cascades, such as this spectacular one at Shoshone Falls. Many of the state's names feature the word "falls," such as Idaho Falls, Twin Falls, and American Falls. The Snake River runs through Hell's Canyon, the deepest gorge in North America and far deeper than the Grand Canyon.

## MOOSE
The largest member of the deer family, the moose lives in northern woodlands near water. With its long legs it can wade through swamps or pick its way through snowy forests. Once moose lived throughout the northern United States, but almost all the moose in the east were killed by hunters. Moose are now protected by law.

## WHITE-WATER RAFTING
A kayak on the Salmon River, which twists and cuts its way through the Salmon River Mountains on its way west to the Snake River. The Salmon is the longest river within any state. River rafters shoot the rapids of this "river of no return"—so called because there is no turning back in the swift current. Such outdoor adventure sports attract thousands of visitors to Idaho's unspoiled acres.

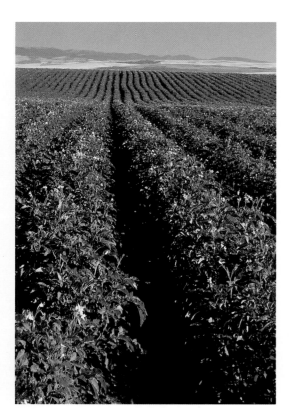

## IDAHO POTATO
No other state compares with Idaho in potato production. The lava-rich soils that drain southward from the Snake River provide fertile growing ground for this important food of the western world. The potato originated in South America and was introduced to North America in the 1600s.

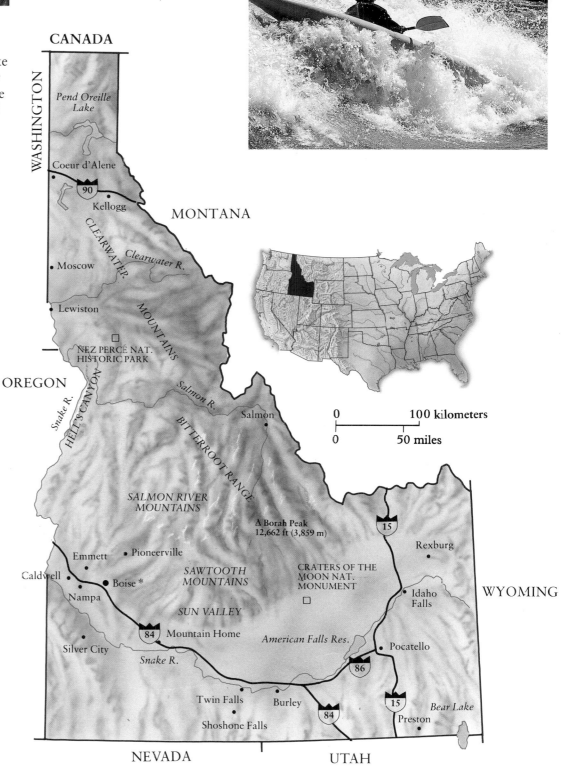

CANADA

WASHINGTON

Pend Oreille Lake

Coeur d'Alene

90

Kellogg

MONTANA

CLEARWATER

Clearwater R.

Moscow

MOUNTAINS

Lewiston

NEZ PERCÉ NAT. HISTORIC PARK

OREGON

Salmon R.

Salmon

HELL'S CANYON

Snake R.

BITTERROOT RANGE

SALMON RIVER MOUNTAINS

▲ Borah Peak 12,662 ft (3,859 m)

Rexburg

Emmett    • Pioneerville

Caldwell

SAWTOOTH MOUNTAINS

CRATERS OF THE MOON NAT. MONUMENT

Idaho Falls

WYOMING

Nampa    • Boise *

SUN VALLEY

84

Mountain Home

American Falls Res.

Silver City

Snake R.

Pocatello

86

Twin Falls    Burley

84

15

Bear Lake

Shoshone Falls

Preston

NEVADA

UTAH

0       100 kilometers

0       50 miles

# ILLINOIS

Located in the heart of the Midwest, Illinois typifies that region's broad, level landscape—which explains its popular name, the "Prairie State." The fertile soil and long growing season make it an important agricultural state. It is among the leading producers of soybeans and corn. Wheat, oats, barley, rye, and sorghum are also grown in large quantities. Hogs, pigs, and cattle are important to the state's economy. Illinois is also a major industrial state; in fact, manufacturing is much more vital to Illinois than farming, and products include electronic equipment and chemicals. Chicago, the largest city in Illinois and home of O'Hare Airport, is a major center for rail and truck transportation, as well as for the Great Lakes shipping traffic. There is mining in the southern part of the state. During the 1800s and early 1900s Illinois' factories and stockyards were the workplaces where many of America's labor unions first formed.

*White oak*

The Mississippi forms the western border of the state from Galena—home of General Ulysses S. Grant and endowed with many restored Victorian buildings—to Cairo in the south. Evidence of Illinois' prehistoric inhabitants is plentiful. There have been dwellers on the plains since 4000 B.C., and a period of burial mound building began after about 1000 B.C. Monk's Mound, one of the Cahokia Mounds, in the southwest of the state near East St. Louis, is the largest Native American mound in the country. The name "Illinois" comes from the tribes that once lived in the area. They called themselves Illinewek, or "superior men." French fur traders were the first European settlers in the early 1600s.

*Cardinal*

STATE SYMBOLS

*Illinois native violet*

## HOME OF LINCOLN
Springfield, near the center of the state, was home to the young lawyer, congressman, and finally president, Abraham Lincoln. The town cemetery holds his tomb. In the village of New Salem there is a state park which honors his time there as a storekeeper, law student, and surveyor.

## CHICAGO SKYLINE
Chicago is the third-largest city in the United States and the birthplace of the skyscraper. The John Hancock Center in the middle of the picture is one of the city's tallest buildings. The Sears Tower (not shown) is the tallest building in North America.

### ILLINOIS

**Capital**
Springfield
**Area**
57,914 sq. mi.
(149,986 sq. km)
**Population**
12,852,548 (2007)
**Largest cities**
Chicago (2,836,658)
Aurora (170,617)
**Statehood**
December 3, 1818
Rank: 21st
**Principal rivers**
Mississippi, Ohio,
Illinois, Wabash
**Highest point**
Charles Mound
1,235 feet (376m)
**Motto**
State Sovereignty—
National Union
**Song**
"Illinois"

## FOOD OF THE FUTURE
A typical farm with its crop of soybeans (foreground) and corn. More soybeans are grown in Illinois than in any other state. The town of Decatur has the label "soybean capital of the world." The soybean is also the second most important crop—after corn—for the whole of the United States. Corn accounts for some 58 percent of total crop produce, while soy makes up almost 15 percent.

## MISSISSIPPI BARGES
Barges with up to 50 containers travel slowly along the Mississippi River, the "Father of Waters," near Cairo in the south of the state. Thus, Chicago serves as a shipping crossroads between the Great Lakes and the Gulf Coast. The Mississippi runs along Illinois' western border. The Illinois River links it to Lake Michigan via the Illinois Waterway.

## WHITE-TAILED DEER
The white-tailed deer is the most common deer in North America. The open country of the Illinois plains suits its habits, and it can run at 40 miles per hour (64km/h) to avoid predators. As with all deer, the male grows antlers. The deer eats leaves, fruit, and grass, as well as the bark of trees.

## CARL SANDBURG
The poet, historian, and folklorist Carl Sandburg was born in Galesburg in 1878. He became famous for his poetic descriptions of gritty American life. Sandburg was a popular folk singer and made a collection of songs, *The American Songbag*, in 1927. He wrote a famous six-volume biography of Abraham Lincoln and also wrote children's books.

# INDIANA

Rich in farmlands, Indiana ranks among the top-ten agricultural states of the Union. It is also an important industrial state. Its motto as "Crossroads of America" is well earned—it is a major Midwest road, rail, river, lake, and canal transportation center. In the northwest it borders Lake Michigan, and this lakefront area has plenty of industry. Shipping carries goods from the lake, via the St. Lawrence Seaway to other U.S. and overseas markets. The Ohio River forms the state's southern border and flows into the Mississippi, allowing the state's produce to be carried on to New Orleans. Farmland makes up 65 percent of the state, and almost 95 percent of Indiana's produce is sent to other parts of the country. Corn is the chief crop, but soybeans and wheat are also grown. Hogs and pigs, cattle, and chickens are raised. There are also valuable tracts of forest.

Industry began in the 1800s with coal mines and quarries, followed by oil refineries, steel mills, and factories, which are concentrated around Gary, Fort Wayne, and South Bend in the north. Indiana's industrialization has caused pollution problems over the years, but laws now attempt to control the damage and safeguard wild areas on Lake Michigan's shoreline. For example, visitors can explore the windswept dunes and forests of the Indiana Dunes National Lakeshore, at the crescent of Lake Michigan. Indiana got its name from the many Native American tribes (mistakenly called "Indians" at the time) that once lived there. In the early 1800s these tribes fought a number of fierce battles with the U.S. Army. At Tippecanoe in 1811 General William Henry Harrison defeated the Miami Native Americans and cleared the way for a permanent European settlement. The nickname "Hoosier" state is harder to attribute. The most likely explanation relates to Samuel Hoosier, who was working on the Ohio Falls Canal in Louisville, Kentucky, in 1826. He preferred to hire men from across the river in Indiana, and "Hoosier's men" came to mean reliable workers, from whom the state may have taken its nickname.

## STATE SYMBOLS

*Tulip tree*

*Cardinal*

*Peony*

**SMELL BARRIER**
Widespread over North America, skunks dwell in dens and burrows over much of Indiana's prairie land. The skunk has two white stripes down its black, furry body, and a thin white line on its face. Its distinctive appearance should warn off most attackers; but should they provoke it they will be overpowered by the fluid it sprays from its tail-end glands. Only owls are serious predators, because they can swoop on skunks before the release of the fluid, which can be sprayed to over 6 feet (2m). Skunks come out chiefly at night to forage.

**CITY OF WHEELS**
In the dead center of the state, Indianapolis is both the state's capital and its largest city. Major highways emerge from the city like spokes from a wheel, and Indianapolis has more major highway connections than any other city in the United States. At the center of the city stands the tall Soldiers and Sailors Monument in World War Memorial Plaza. Nearby is the state capitol building (below).

### INDIANA

**Capital**
Indianapolis
**Area**
36,418 sq. mi.
(94,315 sq. km)
**Population**
6,345,289 (2007)
**Largest cities**
Indianapolis (795,458)
Fort Wayne (251,247)
**Statehood**
December 11, 1816
Rank: 19th
**Principal rivers**
Ohio, Wabash,
White
**Highest point**
Wayne County,
Franklin Township
1,257 feet (383m)
**Motto**
Crossroads of America
**Song**
"On the Banks of the
Wabash, Far Away"

## RACE OF CHAMPIONS

"Gentlemen, start your engines" heralds the start of the annual Indianapolis 500 auto race, held some 5 miles (8km) west of the downtown area. The Motor Speedway track is 2.5 miles (4km) in circumference. The race is held over the Memorial Day weekend, and hundreds of thousands of visitors swell the city for the event. Indianapolis also holds a traditional Memorial Day parade. Visitors to the city can take a special bus ride around the world-famous track and then go on to visit displays of antique race cars.

## WOODCHUCK

The woodchuck is a member of the squirrel family and is found in wooded areas, including the forests of southern Indiana. It is about 25 inches (65cm) long, with a bushy tail and sharp-clawed feet that help it dig its underground burrows: hence its other name of groundhog. It feeds on grass, leaves, shoots, seeds, and fruit.

## MILES OF CORN

Indiana's number-one crop is corn, and this contributes to the state's standing as a top-ten farming producer. There are almost 60,000 farms, which are all highly mechanized. Those farms that belong to the Amish and Mennonite sects, devout Christians who settled in Indiana in the 1800s, preserve older traditions of farming. Their farms are located in the north of the state, around Berne and Goshen. Other crops include sorghum, oats, rye, and hay. Tomatoes, spearmint, and peppermint are all important crops.

## BRIEF OFFICE

William Henry Harrison was the ninth president, but his term of office lasted barely one month in 1841. While delivering his Inaugural Address, he caught a cold that later turned into pneumonia. His success against the Native Americans, particularly at the battle of Tippecanoe, won him the election. He was the president with the shortest term and the first to die in office.

LAKE MICHIGAN
MICHIGAN
Hammond Michigan City
Gary
80 90
South Bend Elkhart
Goshen
INDIANA DUNES NAT. LAKESHORE
Tippecanoe
Fort Wayne
65
Wabash
Mississinewa Lake
69
Berne
Kokomo Marion
ILLINOIS
Wabash R. Lafayette
74
Muncie
Anderson
Noblesville
1,257 ft (383 m) Δ
70
Speedway Indianapolis * Richmond
OHIO
Terre Haute
70
74
White R. Bloomington
Columbus
Vincennes Washington
East Fork R.
65
Ohio R.
New Albany
Lincoln City
Jeffersonville
64
LINCOLN BOYHOOD NAT. MEMORIAL
Evansville
KENTUCKY

0   50 kilometers
0   30 miles

# IOWA

A rich farming state of the Midwest, Iowa competes with Illinois for first place in growing corn, and raises more pigs and hogs than any other state. It ranks third in cattle production. Around 90 percent of the state is farmland. One reason for Iowa's high output of agricultural crops is its gently rolling land: its soil, mostly black loam and rocks, is fertile—deposited by melting glaciers at the end of the last Ice Age. Once the crops and livestock leave the farms they contribute to Iowa's considerable industrial output as factories turn them into meat, cereals, animal feeds, and other processed food products. Farm machinery is another key industry. The eastern border of Iowa is the Mississippi River, while its western border is formed by the Big Sioux and Missouri rivers. The Mississippi and Missouri, which eventually converage just north of St. Louis, Missouri, are important to Iowa as a key agricultural state. These rivers provide irrigation water in case of drought, as well as serving as waterways for shipping bulk goods, such as grain, to other parts of the country.

The first Europeans to see Iowa were probably French explorers and fur trappers. Iowa was part of the land included in the Louisiana Purchase of 1803. In 1832 an uprising of Sauk (or Sac) and Fox tribes, led by Black Hawk, attempted to oust the Europeans but was defeated, and more settlers filled the region. It became a U.S. territory in 1838. Iowa's nickname, "Hawkeye," probably honors Black Hawk.

In Iowa City there is the University of Iowa and the original state capitol, dating from the time when the state was admitted to the Union. Iowa is also home to seven villages called the Amana Colonies, founded in the 1850s. This German religious sect sought religious freedom, and their descendants continue a tradition of making woolens, furniture, wine, and baked goods.

### GILDED DOMES
Iowa's Capitol Building in Des Moines has gold-leafed domes that doninate the surrounding area. The building took 15 years to complete (in 1886). Nearly 30 types of marble went into its ornate construction. Inside the building are murals and mosaics. The annual State Fair is held in Des Moines in August.

*Oak*

STATE SYMBOLS

*Eastern goldfinch*          *Wild rose*

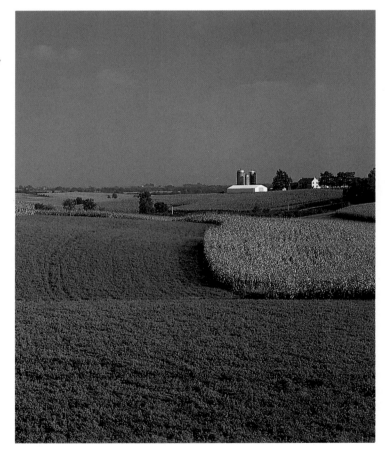

### ALFALFA AND CORN FIELDS
A farm in Iowa with corn and alfalfa crops growing side by side. The state's leading position in farming, both nationally and internationally, is based on the feeding (as well as selling) of livestock. Corn and alfalfa provide important food for cattle. Alfalfa is a plant of the pea family which originated in the Middle East. Today the Midwest states, particularly Iowa, produce the most alfalfa in the world.

### DEPRESSION PRESIDENT
Herbert Clark Hoover was born in West Branch, Iowa, where his birthplace has been restored as a historic site. During his term of office, from 1929 to 1933, the United States experienced the worst economic depression in its history. Hoover was blamed for not doing enough to help the poor and jobless. He died in 1964.

## SOY

Originally from China and Japan, the soybean was introduced to the United States at the start of the 1800s, and established its place in the Midwest. The soya plant is upright and leafy, growing up to 6 feet (2m) high, and lives for only one year. It produces a number of pods, which contain one to four seeds, or beans.

## THE MIGHTY MISSISSIPPI

The Mississippi River runs its powerful course in Guttenberg, on the eastern border of Iowa. Much of the state is rolling—rather than flat—countryside. There are also many bluffs along the river banks of both the Mississippi and Missouri rivers. Bluffs are high, steep banks or cliffs. The Mississippi River irrigates the fertile farms along its banks and provides barge and other boat transportation for the state's farm produce.

```
0    50 kilometers
0    30 miles
```

MINNESOTA

SOUTH DAKOTA

Δ 1,670 ft (509 m)

• Spencer

• Mason City

WISCONSIN

• Sioux City

Fort Dodge •

• Charles City

Guttenburg •

• Storm Lake

Boone •

Cedar Falls • • Waterloo

Dubuque •

Mississippi R.

Big Sioux R.

Missouri R.

Iowa R.

Cedar R.

380

AMANA COLONIES □

• Cedar Rapids

Marshalltown •

Clinton •

NEBRASKA

29

80

80

Des Moines *

• West Branch

Iowa City •

Davenport

Lake Red Rock

Indianola •

Des Moines R.

ILLINOIS

• Council Bluffs

Creston •

• Ottumwa

Burlington •

29

Shenandoah •

35

Fort Madison •

MISSOURI

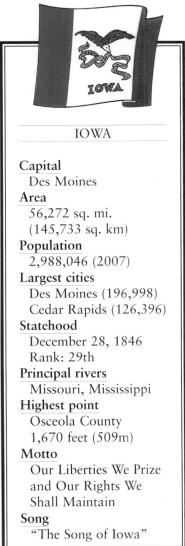

### IOWA

**Capital**
Des Moines
**Area**
56,272 sq. mi.
(145,733 sq. km)
**Population**
2,988,046 (2007)
**Largest cities**
Des Moines (196,998)
Cedar Rapids (126,396)
**Statehood**
December 28, 1846
Rank: 29th
**Principal rivers**
Missouri, Mississippi
**Highest point**
Osceola County
1,670 feet (509m)
**Motto**
Our Liberties We Prize
and Our Rights We
Shall Maintain
**Song**
"The Song of Iowa"

## HOG FARMING

Iowa has often ranked second in terms of overall value of its livestock, and the state produces more than 25 percent of the nation's pigs, with 13.5 million hogs and nearly 30 million pigs. Hogs are pigs that weigh over 120 pounds (50kg). Corn is the pigs' main food, and Iowa produces that, too, in abundance. More than two-thirds of the nation's pigs are raised in the corn belt states of the Midwest. There are almost 59 million pigs on U.S. farms, made up of some 20 breeds. Spotted swine, American landrace, and Poland china are among the breeds raised commercially.

# KANSAS

The state of Kansas lies at the very center of the continental United States. There is a monument to acknowledge this fact just outside Lebanon, Smith County, in north-central Kansas. A few miles from here the state song, "Home on the Range," was written. As with the other Midwest states, farming plays a major part in the Kansas economy, and large farms dominate the flat central plain. The farming wealth of Kansas comes from its rich soil, made fertile over millions of years as it developed out of an inland sea. Wheat, sorghum, and corn are grown on this flat and fertile land. Meat packing is also important. In the east there are rolling hills, and in the west the state steepens slowly to become part of the Great Plains that rise toward the Rocky Mountains. Kansas is a leading wheat growing state. It is also the leading sorghum producer, and the state's grains, along with grains from other states, are stored in huge grain silos. There are 200 million bushels of grain held in the storage silos of Wichita and Topeka. Both these cities are also heavily industrialized.

The Spanish explorer Francisco Vásquez de Coronado was the first European to see Kansas, while searching unsuccessfully for gold in 1541. There were also many Native American tribes in the region, including Wichita, Pawnee, Osage, and Kansa—from which the state gets its name. Kansas formed part of the Louisiana Purchase of 1803, when Napoleon sold his North American territories to President Thomas Jefferson. In 1825 a treaty was made to allow safe passage across Osage Native American land for pioneers taking their wagons on the Santa Fe Trail. Two years later the first army post west of the Mississippi, at Fort Leavenworth, was opened to protect both settlers and pioneers from Native American attacks. Before the Civil War the state became the scene of such violence between pro- and anti-slavery groups that it was called "Bleeding Kansas." Kansas developed quickly after the Civil War, especially as the railroad came to Wichita, Abilene, and Dodge City—centers of the "Wild West." Soon cowboys were driving cattle up from Texas to catch these railheads. Kansas has been a leading state in developing women's political rights. Susanna Salter became the country's first woman mayor in 1987.

Western meadowlark

Cottonwood

**STATE SYMBOLS**

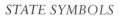

Sunflower

## KANSAS

**Capital**
Topeka
**Area**
82,277 sq. mi.
(213,081 sq. km)
**Population**
2,775,997 (2007)
**Largest cities**
Wichita (354,865)
Overland Park (164,811)
**Statehood**
January 29, 1861
Rank: 34th
**Principal rivers**
Kansas, Republican,
Smoky Hill, Arkansas
**Highest point**
Mt. Sunflower
4,039 feet (1,232m)
**Motto**
*Ad Astra per Aspera*
(To the Stars through
Difficulties)
**Song**
"Home on the Range"

WHERE THE BUFFALO ROAM
Millions of American bison—usually called buffalo, although they are not true buffalo—once roamed the Midwest plains and prairies. They were hunted by Native Americans. Later white hunters using rifles slaughtered some 50 million bison. Today they are protected in national parks.

AIR CAPITAL
Kansas is a leading state in the manufacture of aircraft. Wichita owes much of its past growth to its aircraft industry. Commerical, private, and military planes have been made here—among them such well-known names as Boeing, Lear, and Cessna. This picture shows Lear jets in production. There is also a major air force base in Wichita.

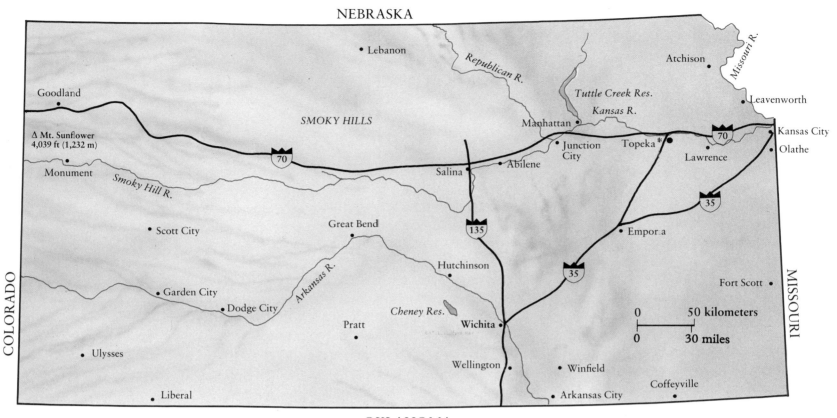

NEBRASKA

Lebanon

Goodland

*Republican R.*

Atchison

*SMOKY HILLS*

*Tuttle Creek Res.*

*Kansas R.*

Manhattan

Leavenworth

Δ Mt. Sunflower
4,039 ft (1,232 m)

70

Topeka *

70

Kansas City

Monument

*Smoky Hill R.*

Salina

Junction
City

Lawrence

Olathe

Abilene

COLORADO

Scott City

Great Bend

135

Emporia

35

Hutchinson

35

Fort Scott

MISSOURI

Garden City

*Arkansas R.*

Dodge City

*Cheney Res.*

Pratt

Wichita

0      50 kilometers

0      30 miles

Ulysses

Wellington

Winfield

Coffeyville

Liberal

Arkansas City

OKLAHOMA

## MONUMENT ROCKS

Modern reminders of the Ice Age glaciers that once swept over the plains and covered most of Kansas, these oddly-shaped formations are called Monument Rocks. They are situated near Scott City and are over 10,000 years old.

## GRAIN HARVEST

Kansas ranks second among the states in wheat production. Its soil is among the most fertile in the world, and tall grain elevators and combines are common sights on the flat, rural landscape. Wheat farming on a large scale really took off in the 1880s, after the ranching cattle boom died down.

## PILOT AND PIONEER

The famous American aviator Amelia Earhart was born in Kansas in 1897. She became the first woman to fly alone across the Atlantic in 1932. In 1937 she and a navigator attempted to fly around the world, but her plane was lost in the Pacific Ocean with less than one-third of her journey to finish.

## COWBOY COUNTRY

Dodge City, in the southwest of the state, has many restored store fronts, saloons, wagons, and stagecoaches from its infamous Wild West frontier days. During the 1870s and 1880s longhorn cattle were driven up from Texas by cowboys to the railroad here. The city also attracted businessmen, cattle rustlers, stagecoach robbers, and saloon belles. Frontiersmen such as Wyatt Earp and Doc Holliday once strolled along the boardwalks of this cowboy capital.

# KENTUCKY

Situated between the South and the Midwest, Kentucky is the oldest state west of the Appalachians—a mountain chain that has dominated both the state's geography and its history. Nearly one fourth of the state is part of the Appalachian Plateau—also called the Eastern Coal Field.

The Appalachians formed a barrier to westward expansion for the original 13 Atlantic seaboard colonies. People knew that there was land to the west, but getting past the mountains was the problem. The best-known pioneer was Daniel Boone, who blazed the Wilderness Trail through what is now called Cumberland Gap in the mountains in 1775. The area is now part of the Cumberland Gap National Historic park (shared with Tennessee and Virginia). With 20,222 acres (8,190 hectares) it is the nation's largest historic park. The gap is a natural break about 800 feet (245m) below the peaks. Nearby, Pinnacle Overlook has commanding views of the mountains and valleys. The borders of the three states meet at Tri-State Peak. The Daniel Boone National Forest contains the Red River Gorge. After Boone's exploration, many white settlers followed, clearing trees and farming hemp, corn, hogs, rye, and tobacco. Today tobacco, soybeans, wheat, and bluegrass are among the leading crops.

Bluegrass, from which the state gets its nickname, has bluish-green blades and is a food source for livestock and for the famous horses of Kentucky. The state ranks first in the breeding of thoroughbred horses, and the Kentucky Derby is held each year in Louisville. "Bluegrass" is also a term used to describe the local country music. One product for which the state is famous worldwide is Kentucky bourbon whiskey—a drink that is made from corn. Other manufactured items include trucks and automobiles, food products, and chemicals. Kentucky was the birthplace of the two opposing Civil War presidents—the Union's Abraham Lincoln and the Confederacy's Jefferson Davis.

*Kentucky coffee tree*

*Goldenrod*

STATE SYMBOLS

*Cardinal*

KENTUCKY COAL
Kentucky leads the nation in total coal production. There are many mines in the hilly eastern part of the state, in the Appalachian plateau. The coal mined in this area is a hardened, highly-valued variety called anthracite, which is widely used in industry. Much of the region has suffered from the effects of strip mining and large-scale felling of trees. This is now controlled by law, but much damage remains. Other minerals in the state include petroleum, natural, gas, and iron ore.

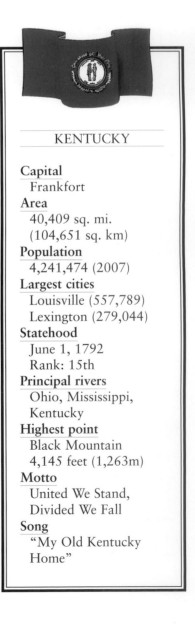

| KENTUCKY | |
|---|---|
| **Capital** | Frankfort |
| **Area** | 40,409 sq. mi. (104,651 sq. km) |
| **Population** | 4,241,474 (2007) |
| **Largest cities** | Louisville (557,789) Lexington (279,044) |
| **Statehood** | June 1, 1792 Rank: 15th |
| **Principal rivers** | Ohio, Mississippi, Kentucky |
| **Highest point** | Black Mountain 4,145 feet (1,263m) |
| **Motto** | United We Stand, Divided We Fall |
| **Song** | "My Old Kentucky Home" |

CUMBERLAND FALLS
These impressive falls, also known as Great Falls, are part of the Cumberland River, which flows through eastern Kentucky and Tennessee. They drop 68 feet (21m). The river frequently floods in winter and spring, but it is low-level in summer. It flows on to the Ohio River. The Cumberland Gap, Plateau, Falls, and River were all named after the Duke of Cumberland, the son of King George I of England.

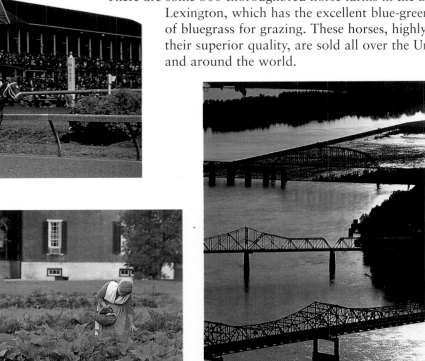

## THE KENTUCKY DERBY

One of the most famous horse races in the world is the Kentucky Derby. It is held every year on the first Saturday in May in Churchill Downs, Louisville. There are some 300 thoroughbred horse farms in the area around Lexington, which has the excellent blue-green pastures of bluegrass for grazing. These horses, highly prized for their superior quality, are sold all over the United States and around the world.

## "THE GREATEST"

Native Kentuckian Muhammad Ali (originally named Cassius Clay) was born in Lexington in 1942. He is the only boxer to win the world heavyweight title three times. He won an Olympic Gold Medal in 1960, and went on to dominate boxing, calling himself "the Greatest."

## TRADITIONAL WAYS

The Shakers are a small religious sect who follow a very simple way of life. This is reflected in their traditional farming methods and particularly in their distinctive furniture, which is world famous for its simple, well-made shapes. The Shaker village in Pleasant Hill was established in the 1800s. The Shakers stopped accepting converts in the 1960s. As they do not believe in marriage or child bearing, instead relying on conversion and adoptions, their numbers are now extremely low.

## OHIO RIVER

To the north of the state, the Ohio River separates Kentucky from Ohio, Indiana, and Illinois. The river is itself a tributary of the Mississippi, and more water flows from it into the Mississippi than from any other tributary.

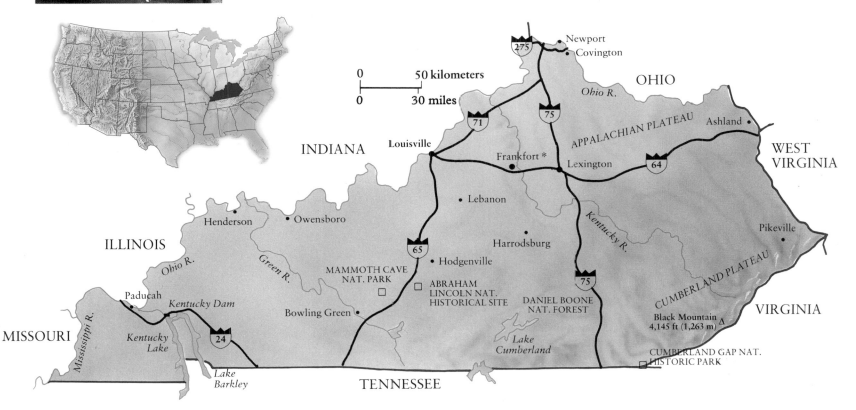

# LOUISIANA

Located on the Gulf of Mexico, Louisiana is the lowest-lying state, averaging only 100 feet (30m) above sea level. Its flatness causes problems along the Gulf coast, which is below sea level and requires dikes, levees, and pumping stations to protect against flooding. It is also mainly rural, with large areas of swamps and sluggish marshes called bayous. Many pelicans live in these marshes and give Louisiana its nickname. The Mississippi River has played an important role in the state's history and economy. Louisiana's three largest cities—New Orleans, Baton Rouge, and Shreveport—are all located on the river. The river forms part of the state's eastern border with the state of Mississippi, before entering Mississippi Delta. Louisiana's industry includes petroleum and natural gas (located off the coast), ranking second only to Texas in production. It is also the number one salt-producing state. Soybeans, sugarcane, and rice are the leading crops. Louisiana leads all other states in its fishing industry, consisting mainly of shellfish.

Louisiana's culture is unique, mainly because of its French origins. Although the Spanish explorer Hernando de Soto sailed there in 1541, the region was claimed for France in 1682 by La Salle. The whole area eventually formed the Louisiana Purchase of 1803. Early French and Spanish settlers were known as Creoles, and their culture is still strong. So too is Cajun cooking, music, and language—the legacy of some 4,000 French people forcibly relocated in the late 1700s by the British from Acadia in Nova Scotia, Canada. The word "Acadian" became shortened to Cajun. Additionally, many Africans were brought to Louisiana in the 1700s and 1800s as slaves, both from Africa and via the Caribbean.

In 2005, Hurricane Katrina devastated the city of New Orleans, breaching the levee system and flooding 80 percent of the city. The death toll exceeded 1,800, making it the deadliest hurricane in almost 100 years and the costliest in U.S. history. The city of New Orleans is still undergoing major rebuilding following this catastrophic event.

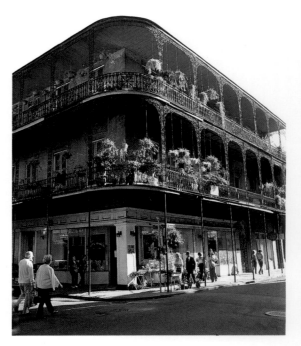

## NEW ORLEANS
This city is unlike any other in the United States. Its ornate wrought-ironwork balconies are an attractive feature on the many buildings from the Spanish and French colonial era. New Orleans is famous for its French Quarter, with restaurants serving spicy Creole cooking and entertainers performing in the streets. Its many cafés offer the traditional half chicory coffee, half hot milk drink.

## DIXIELAND JAZZ
The French Quarter of New Orleans is considered the birthplace of jazz—a form of music developed from a mixture of African and Southern influences. Here in the early 1900s the first jazz marching bands played then moved indoors to clubs, restaurants, and halls, such as Preservation Hall. One of the great jazz trumpeters and singers, Louis Armstrong (third from left in the picture), played with King Oliver's Creole Jazz band in the 1920s in New Orleans.

*Brown pelican*

STATE
SYMBOLS

*Bald cypress*

## FRENCH FOUNDER
French explorer Robert Cavelier Sieur de La Salle sailed down the Mississippi with a party of French and Native Americans. On April 9, 1682, on reaching the mouth of the river, he claimed all the land in the Mississippi Basin for France. He called the land Louisiana after the French king, Louis XIV. La Salle was the first European to travel the length of the Mississippi River. In 1684 he returned to the Americas to found a colony at the river's mouth, but he was murdered by mutineers before he reached the Mississippi.

*Magnolia*

## LOUISIANA

**Capital**
Baton Rouge
**Area**
51,840 sq. mi.
(134,255 sq. km)
**Population**
4,293,204 (2007)
**Largest cities**
New Orleans (275,000)
Baton Rouge (227,071)
**Statehood**
April 30, 1812
Rank: 18th
**Principal rivers**
Mississippi, Red,
Sabine
**Highest point**
Driskill Mountain
535 feet (163m)
**Motto**
Union, Justice,
and Confidence
**Song**
"Give Me Louisiana"

### MARDI GRAS

February (or sometimes March) is the time for Mardi Gras, which is French for "Fat Tuesday" and refers to the custom of using up all the fats in the home before Lent begins. Its origins lie in the Roman Catholic tradition of celebrating the day before Ash Wednesday, the beginning of Lent. In New Orleans this has become an extravagant parade of costumed merrymakers dancing, singing, and marching through the streets.

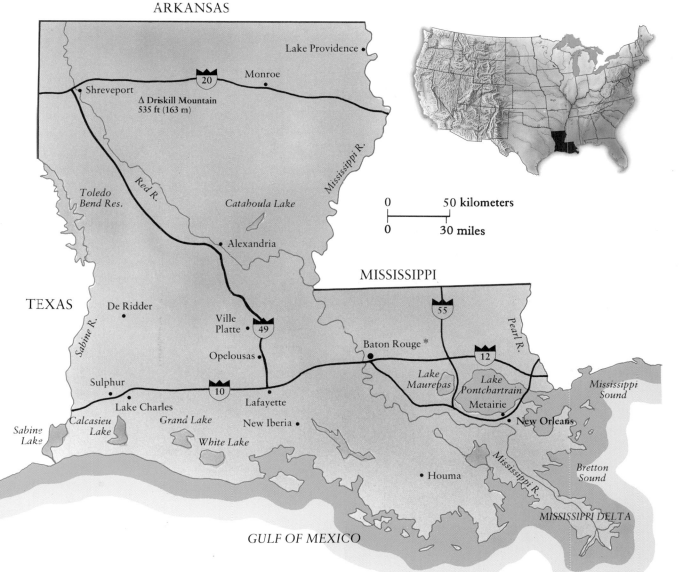

### SOURCES OF SULFUR

Hot liquid sulfur spews out of a pipe from a mine in the aptly named town of Sulphur. Sulfur, or sulphur, is found in large deposits along the coast of the Gulf of Mexico. It is located in salt deposits that are drilled from special wells. Some sulfur is extracted from below the ocean floor. Other sulfur is recovered from the mining of natural gas and oil. It is stored in huge vats. Sulfur is an industrial mineral that is used in many compounds.

### CRAYFISH COOKING

Louisiana is the leading state in commercial fishing, especially shellfish. Most of the catch is exported to other parts of the United States, but there is also a strong tradition of local seafood cooking, particularly with crayfish. The crayfish is related to the lobster, and both are caught near the shore. Many are caught in freshwater lakes and swamps by bayou shrimp boats.

# MAINE

The most easterly of all the states in the continental U.S., Maine is also the largest state in New England. It forms the northeastern corner of the United States, and is bordered by the Canadian provinces of New Brunswick and Quebec, as well as by New Hampshire. The state has a long and rocky coastline on the Atlantic Ocean. Maine is a thinly populated state. It was originally part of Massachusetts but broke away in 1820. The state is naturally divided into two types of landscapes—the coastal lowlands and the mountain plateau. The rugged, tree-lined coast has plenty of bays, sandy beaches, and natural harbors, which make it ideal for fishing. Maine seafood, especially lobster, is world famous. Herring and cod are also important catches. Sport fishermen are attracted by sea bass, salmon, and trout. Maine grows enough potatoes to be counted among the top producers in the country of this vegetable. Other crops include corn, hay, blueberries, and apples. Paper production is the leading industry. Footwear, electrical and electronic equipment, machinery, and textiles are other important manufactured goods.

Tourists come to view the rugged and rock-bound coastline, as well as the wildlife in the many national parks, including the Rachel Carson Wildlife Refuge. Carson was a nature writer who warned of environmental dangers. She lived in Kennebunkport, a summer resort that also boasts the summer house of George Bush, Sr. It is possible that the Vikings may have reached Maine as far back as A.D. 1000. John Cabot explored the coast for England in 1498—only six years after Columbus' first voyage to the New World.

*STATE SYMBOLS*

*Chickadee*

*Eastern white pine*

*White pine cone & tassel*

**FARMLAND**
Situated in the center of Maine, the forest highlands of Baxter State Park from the Backdrop to this rolling farmland and typical New England village, with its single-spired churches. There is no large-scale farming in the state, but potatoes are grown in this region, as are apples, blueberries, and other fruits. Mt. Katahdin, the state's highest peak, is situated in Baxter State Park. The northern end of the Appalachian Trail is also located there, and the area attracts hikers and campers.

**AUGUSTA**
The state capital, Augusta, is a dynamic city. Here a boat race further enlivens the busy riverfront. The city is the hub of commerce and industry. Plymouth colonists established a fort here in 1628. A later fort, Fort Western (1754), has been restored for visitors.

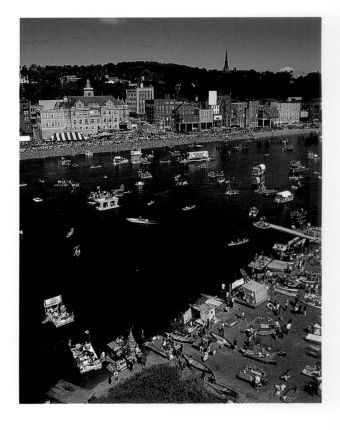

**LIGHTHOUSE**
Maine's coastline is dotted with old lighthouses, such as Nubble Lighthouse on Cape Neddick, which were built to warn clippers and whalers away from the perilous rocky shore. It is also along this shoreline that the most easterly point in the United States is located: at West Quoddy Head, a small peninsula near Lubec.

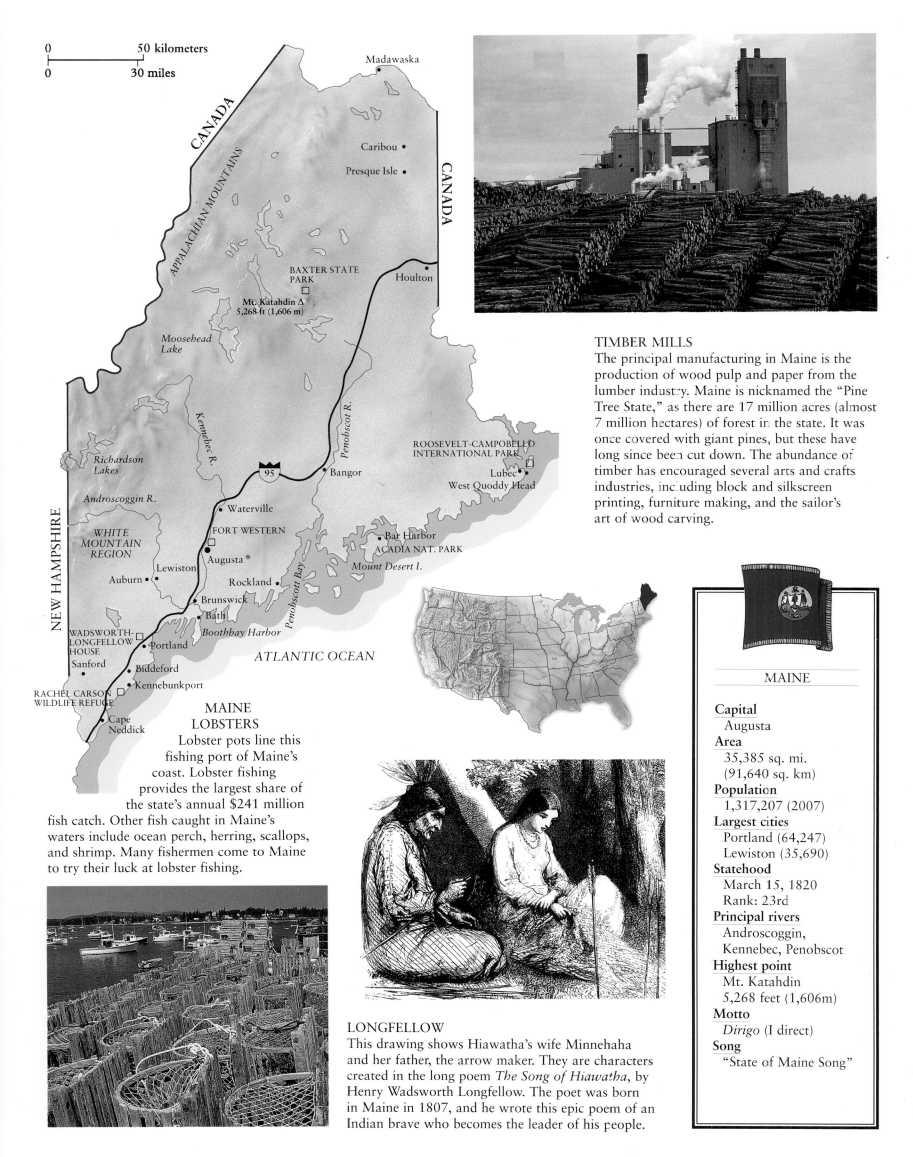

0    50 kilometers
0    30 miles

**CANADA**

Madawaska

**APPALACHIAN MOUNTAINS**

Caribou

Presque Isle

**CANADA**

BAXTER STATE
PARK

Houlton

Mt. Katahdin △
5,268 ft (1,606 m)

Moosehead
Lake

Penobscot R.

Kennebec R.

ROOSEVELT-CAMPOBELLO
INTERNATIONAL PARK

Richardson
Lakes

95

Bangor

Lubec
West Quoddy Head

Androscoggin R.

Waterville

**WHITE
MOUNTAIN
REGION**

FORT WESTERN

Augusta *

Auburn   Lewiston

Rockland

Bar Harbor
ACADIA NAT. PARK

Brunswick

Penobscot Bay

Mount Desert I.

Bath

Boothbay Harbor

**NEW HAMPSHIRE**

WADSWORTH-
LONGFELLOW
HOUSE

Portland

Sanford

Biddeford

*ATLANTIC OCEAN*

Kennebunkport

RACHEL CARSON
WILDLIFE REFUGE

Cape
Neddick

## TIMBER MILLS

The principal manufacturing in Maine is the production of wood pulp and paper from the lumber industry. Maine is nicknamed the "Pine Tree State," as there are 17 million acres (almost 7 million hectares) of forest in the state. It was once covered with giant pines, but these have long since been cut down. The abundance of timber has encouraged several arts and crafts industries, including block and silkscreen printing, furniture making, and the sailor's art of wood carving.

## MAINE LOBSTERS

Lobster pots line this fishing port of Maine's coast. Lobster fishing provides the largest share of the state's annual $241 million fish catch. Other fish caught in Maine's waters include ocean perch, herring, scallops, and shrimp. Many fishermen come to Maine to try their luck at lobster fishing.

## LONGFELLOW

This drawing shows Hiawatha's wife Minnehaha and her father, the arrow maker. They are characters created in the long poem *The Song of Hiawatha*, by Henry Wadsworth Longfellow. The poet was born in Maine in 1807, and he wrote this epic poem of an Indian brave who becomes the leader of his people.

### MAINE

**Capital**
Augusta
**Area**
35,385 sq. mi.
(91,640 sq. km)
**Population**
1,317,207 (2007)
**Largest cities**
Portland (64,247)
Lewiston (35,690)
**Statehood**
March 15, 1820
Rank: 23rd
**Principal rivers**
Androscoggin,
Kennebec, Penobscot
**Highest point**
Mt. Katahdin
5,268 feet (1,606m)
**Motto**
*Dirigo* (I direct)
**Song**
"State of Maine Song"

# MARYLAND

A Mid-Atlantic state, Maryland is divided into two parts—the Eastern and Western shores—by Chesapeake Bay. Although it is one of the smallest states, its households are the wealthiest in the U.S. Its highly urbanized areas of Baltimore and the suburbs of Washington, D.C., both on the Western Shore, contribute to that prosperity. Most of the state's income comes from manufacturing electric and electronic equipment, chemicals, and food processing. Maryland is also a state of great natural diversity, despite its small size. The Chesapeake Bay and Atlantic coastline contrast sharply with the river valleys, mountains, forests, and rolling hills of the interior.

Maryland was first explored by Captain John Smith in 1608. Twenty-four years later, in 1632, King Charles I gave this land to George Calvert, Lord Baltimore, whose son Cecil founded the first settlement, St. Mary's City, in 1634. He named the colony in honor of Queen Henrietta Maria and established it as a place where his fellow Roman Catholics could enjoy freedom of worship. Members of other faiths were also welcomed—their rights guaranteed by an "Act Concerning Religion," passed in 1649, which made Maryland the first colony to officially practice religious toleration.

Although little of the fighting in the Revolutionary War took place in Maryland, its "troops of the line" fought with special valor, earning praise from General Washington and so giving the state its nickname of the "Old Line State." In the War of 1812 the British bombardment of Fort McHenry, in Baltimore Harbor, inspired Francis Scott Key (imprisoned on a British ship) to write the words of "The Star-Spangled Banner."

Although Maryland was a slave state, it was never dominated by large plantations, and it remained in the Union during the Civil War. It also witnessed some of the fiercest fighting of the war. The Battle of Antietam, near Hagerstown, was one of the bloodiest—over 23,000 men were killed.

Annapolis, the capital, has the oldest state capitol (1779) still in use. It is also the site of the United States Naval Academy. President Jimmy Carter was one of its graduates.

## MARYLAND

**Capital**
Annapolis
**Area**
12,407 sq. mi.
(32,132 sq. km)
**Population**
5,618,344 (2007)
**Largest cities**
Baltimore (637,455)
Columbia (97,200)
**Statehood**
April 28, 1788
Rank: 7th
**Principal rivers**
Susquehanna, Potomac
**Highest point**
Backbone Mountain
3,360 feet (1,024m)
**Motto**
*Fatti Maschii, Parole Femine* (Manly Deeds, Womanly Words)
**Song**
"Maryland, my Maryland"

### BABE RUTH
George Herman "Babe" Ruth was one of baseball's best-loved stars. He was born in 1895 in Baltimore (his birthplace is open to visitors). Babe Ruth began his professional career as a pitcher in 1920, but it was for batting that he was famous. He hit a career total of 714 home runs, unbeaten until 1974.

*STATE SYMBOLS*

*Baltimore oriole*

*White oak*

### CHESAPEAKE BAY
An important inlet of the Atlantic Ocean, Chesapeake Bay splits Maryland in two. The bay is 200 miles (320km) long and is surrounded by Virginia and Maryland. "Chesapeake" is an Algonquian word meaning "country on a big river." The Susquehanna, the Potomac, and several other rivers run into the bay. Baltimore, Maryland, and Norfolk, Virginia, are the two most important ports on the bay. With its many inlets, the bay is a popular vacation spot, offering excellent sailing and fishing. It provides both Maryland and Virginia with an abundance of seafood, especially crabs and oysters.

*Black-eyed Susan*

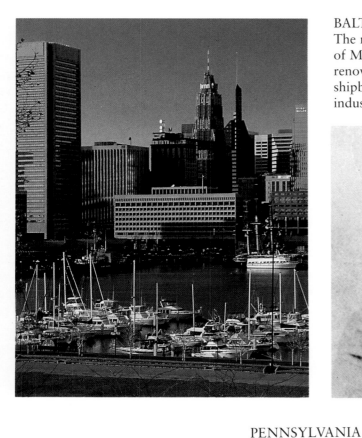

**BALTIMORE**
The most important city of Maryland, Baltimore is renowned as a seaport and shipbuilding center and industrial base.

**MARYLAND CRABS**
Crabs form a large part of Maryland's fishing industry. Fishing in the state's tidal waters for crabs and other species is a favorite pastime and requires no license. Maryland restaurants are renowned for their crab dishes.

**HARRIET TUBMAN**
Born a slave in 1820 in Maryland, Harriet Tubman was called "The Moses of her People" because she helped fellow slaves escape the plantations along the Underground Railroad. This was not a real railroad but a code name for an escape route. She helped over 300 escape.

**TOBACCO HARVEST**
Tobacco is grown widely in Maryland, mainly in the southern part of the Western Shore. After the tobacco is picked, as shown here, it goes to the loose-leaf tobacco auctions in the state, which are the largest in the world. Other Maryland crops are corn, soybeans, melons, apples, and peaches. About 40 percent of the land is cultivated. The Eastern Shore is known for its poultry, eggs, and market gardening. Another 40 percent of the land is forested and so timber is also a major industry.

0 kilometers 50
0 miles 30

# MASSACHUSETTS

Located on the northeastern coast of the United States, the New England state of Massachusetts is bordered on the north by Vermont and New Hampshire. It is one of the smallest states, being only 47 miles (76km) from north to south at its western end, but it has more inhabitants than any other New England state. Most of the people live in the Greater Boston area. The state is steeped in colonial and revolutionary history. The second permanent English settlement (after Jamestown, Virginia) was established there in Plymouth by the Pilgrims in 1620. It was these Pilgrims who started the American celebration of Thanksgiving Day. The Boston Massacre and Boston Tea Party took place there, and the first shots of the Revolutionary War rang out in Lexington and Concord in 1775. Benjamin Franklin, John Adams, and Paul Revere were all born in Massachusetts.

In the center of the state lies rich farmland irrigated by the Connecticut River, which flows north to south. These farms produce cranberries and many vegetables, as well as milk and eggs. West of the river are the beautiful Berkshire Hills that border New York State. Massachusetts is a major industrial state, and witnessed the start of the country's industrial revolution with the establishment of the nation's first textile factory in Waltham in the 1800s. Today, the state's factories produce textiles that are shipped throughout the entire country, as well as electric and electronic equipment, metal products, books, and other printed materials. The state also has a large fishing industry with catches of haddock, flounder, cod, and clams. Massachusetts is famous for its educational establishments, including Harvard University and M.I.T. (Massachusetts Institute of Technology). It is also a major tourist attraction for its historic sites and popular coastal resorts.

*American elm*

STATE SYMBOLS

*Chickadee*

*Mayflower*

SUSAN B. ANTHONY
Born to a Quaker family in Adams, Massachusetts, in 1820, Susan B. Anthony became a teacher and fought for a number of causes, including the anti-slavery campaign. She is best known as a driving force in the early movement for women's rights. She died in 1906, just fourteen years before women gained the right to vote.

FIRST U.S. COLLEGE
Harvard University, located in Cambridge, Massachusetts, was founded in 1636. It was named after a Puritan minister, John Harvard, who left to the college his books and considerable funds. This library is now the largest of any U.S. university, with over 10 million books. Six American presidents were educated there, including Franklin D. Roosevelt and John F. Kennedy. Other graduates include Ralph Waldo Emerson, T. S. Eliot, and Norman Mailer. Harvard was founded as a liberal arts and theological college, but it later widened its scope.

THE BOSTON MASSACRE
On March 5, 1770, angry colonists gathered outside the Customs House in Boston and protested against the presence of British troops in the city. They taunted the British guards with cries of "lobster backs" (after the red coat of a soldier on duty) and hurled snowballs. More soldiers arrived with fixed bayonets, and one soldier opened fire. Five colonists were shot. The resulting "massacre," as it came to be called, was a key event in the developments leading to the Revolutionary War.

VERMONT  NEW HAMPSHIRE

NEW YORK

△ Mt. Greylock
3,491 ft (1,064 m)

Pittsfield

BERKSHIRE
HILLS

Northampton

Fitchburg

Leominster

Amherst

*Quabbin Res.*

Worcester

Holyoke

Southbridge

Springfield

Webster

Millford

*Connecticut R.*

*Merrimack R.*

Lowell

Concord

Lexington

Waltham

Newton

Framingham

Havrhill
Lawrence
Andover

MINUTE MAN NAT.
HISTORIC PARK

Cambridge

Boston *

Quincy

Brockton

Taunton

Fall River

New Bedford

Woods Hole

Rockport
Gloucester

Salem

*Massachusetts Bay*

Plymouth

*Cape Cod Bay*

CAPE COD NAT.
SEASHORE

Provincetown

Yarmouth

*Nantucket Sound*

ATLANTIC OCEAN

*Elizabeth Is.*

*Martha's Vineyard*

*Nantucket I.*

*Buzzard's Bay*

CONNECTICUT  RHODE ISLAND

0 — 50 kilometers
0 — 30 miles

## THE LURE OF CAPE COD
Cape Cod is a large peninsula that hooks around like a curled finger for 65 miles (105km) into the Atlantic Ocean. This aerial view shows Provincetown at the top, with the sandy beach where the Pilgrims first touched land in the foreground. South of it are the Atlantic island resorts of Martha's Vineyard, Nantucket Island, and the Elizabeth Islands. Tourists are a major source of income for the state, and many visitors are drawn there by the beauty of the Cape Cod National Seashore.

## CULTURAL CENTER
Boston is the 20th-largest city in the United States, nonetheless many regard it as the first seat of learning, culture, and the arts. It is unrivaled for its preserved colonial attractions, including the site of the Boston Massacre, Benjamin Franklin's birthplace, and Paul Revere's house. In the 1800s Boston was a great port and industrial center. Today it is home to the Boston Symphony Orchestra and the Museum of Fine Arts. It also serves the needs of thousands of college students and its own residents. Summer days lure much of this population to Boston Common, a thriving hub of recreational activities.

## CRANBERRIES
The cranberry bogs, shallow marshes on Cape Cod, make Massachusetts the leading cranberry producer. Farmers flood the bogs each winter to protect the crops from frost.

### MASSACHUSETTS

**Capital**
Boston
**Area**
10,555 sq. mi.
(27,335 sq. km)
**Population**
6,449,755 (2007)
**Largest cities**
Boston (590,763)
Worcester (175,898)
**Statehood**
February 6, 1788
Rank: 6th
**Principal rivers**
Connecticut, Charles
**Highest point**
Mt. Greylock
3,491 feet (1,064m)
**Motto**
*Ense Petit Placidam Sub Libertate Quietem* (By the Sword We Seek Peace, but Peace Only Under Liberty)
**Song**
"All Hail to Massachusetts"

# MICHIGAN

The state of Michigan is made up of two peninsulas facing each other across the waters of Lake Michigan. The Upper Peninsula and Lower Peninsula, as they are called, do not in fact touch but are linked by the 5-mile (8-km) long Straits of Mackinac Toll Bridge. The state also borders three other Great Lakes—Superior, Huron, and Erie. The Lower Peninsula, which has been dubbed the "mitten" because of its shape, faces a strip of Canadian territory across Lake Huron—the only point where Canada lies directly south of the United States. Mackinaw City stands at the northern end of the end of the "mitten," at the Straits of Mackinac.

Michigan's origins go back to the 1600s, when the French were settling in this area. The state's nickname derives from the great number of wolverines caught by French fur trappers. In 1641, Father Jacques Marquette, a French missionary and explorer, founded a trading post and mission, the first permanent European settlement in Michigan, at Sault Ste. Marie. At this time Michigan was still home to the Ojibwa (Chippewa), Ottawa, and Menominee tribes.

The largest city is Detroit, founded by Antoine de la Mothe, Sieur de Cadillac, in 1701. The city is famous today for its automobile industry and "Motown" music of the 1960s. Detroit is where most American cars and other motor vehicles are designed and manufactured. Various other industries, including defense, space, and food processing are located around Detroit.

The Upper Peninsula is a beautiful land of lakes and pine forests. Sawmills and fishing provide some industry, but this area is mainly a vacation spot, attracting campers, canoeists, and hikers. The climate in this region is very cold in the winter. Michigan is proud of being the "Great Lakes State," as the license plates proclaim. It has 3,121 miles (5,023km) of shoreline, longer than the Atlantic coast from Maine to Florida. It also has 11,000 inland lakes and thousands of waterways.

*White pine*

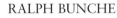

*Robin*

STATE SYMBOLS

*Apple blossom*

DETROIT
The 73-story Renaissance Center complex in downtown Detroit reflects the city's revived fortunes. The covered walkway is part of a nearly 3-mile (5-km) long "People Mover." The city also boasts a symphony orchestra and is the original home of the black "soul" music label Motown Records.

RALPH BUNCHE
One of Michigan's most prestigious sons, Ralph Bunche was born in Detroit in 1904. He studied at UCLA and Harvard and in London and South Africa. Colonialism was his special field. Bunche became a statesman and diplomat, renowned for his negotiating skills. He played an important role in setting up the United Nations and held several important posts in that organization. He won the 1950 Nobel Peace Prize for securing an Arab-Israeli settlement. He died in 1971.

LAKE MICHIGAN
Lake Michigan is the only one of the five Great Lakes to lie entirely within the boundaries of the United States. Apart from Michigan, the other states that surround it are Illinois, Indiana, and Wisconsin. It is the third-largest of the Great Lakes, measuring 321 miles (517km) from north to south and 118 miles (190km) from east to west. It is also the fifth-largest freshwater lake in the world. The lake joins Lake Huron at the Straits of Mackinac, where Michigan's two peninsulas almost meet. The most important of Michigan's ports on the lake is Escanaba. Iron ore leaves Escanaba bound for the steel mills of Gary, Indiana. Fisheries are important, but there are serious pollution problems at the southern tip of the lake.

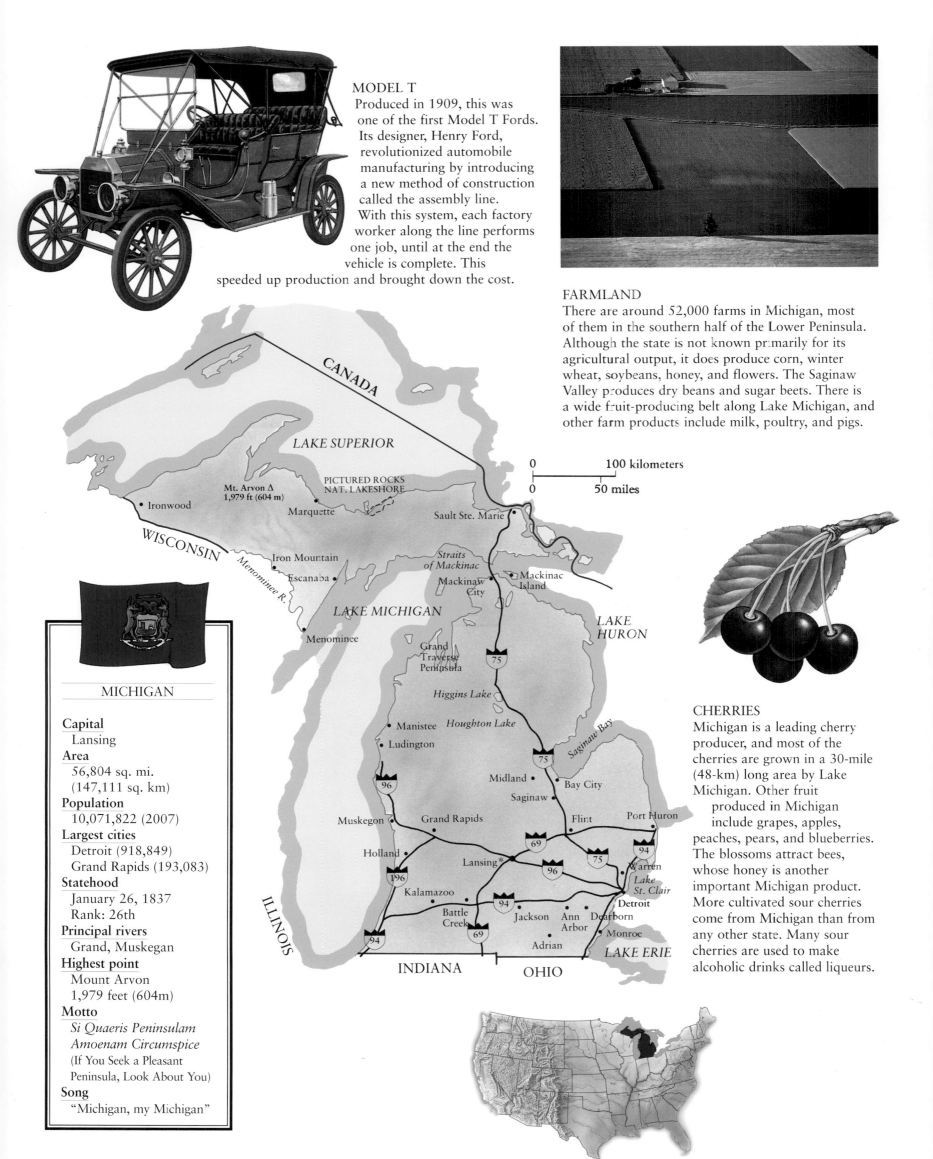

MODEL T
Produced in 1909, this was one of the first Model T Fords. Its designer, Henry Ford, revolutionized automobile manufacturing by introducing a new method of construction called the assembly line. With this system, each factory worker along the line performs one job, until at the end the vehicle is complete. This speeded up production and brought down the cost.

FARMLAND
There are around 52,000 farms in Michigan, most of them in the southern half of the Lower Peninsula. Although the state is not known primarily for its agricultural output, it does produce corn, winter wheat, soybeans, honey, and flowers. The Saginaw Valley produces dry beans and sugar beets. There is a wide fruit-producing belt along Lake Michigan, and other farm products include milk, poultry, and pigs.

CHERRIES
Michigan is a leading cherry producer, and most of the cherries are grown in a 30-mile (48-km) long area by Lake Michigan. Other fruit produced in Michigan include grapes, apples, peaches, pears, and blueberries. The blossoms attract bees, whose honey is another important Michigan product. More cultivated sour cherries come from Michigan than from any other state. Many sour cherries are used to make alcoholic drinks called liqueurs.

**MICHIGAN**

**Capital**
Lansing
**Area**
56,804 sq. mi.
(147,111 sq. km)
**Population**
10,071,822 (2007)
**Largest cities**
Detroit (918,849)
Grand Rapids (193,083)
**Statehood**
January 26, 1837
Rank: 26th
**Principal rivers**
Grand, Muskegan
**Highest point**
Mount Arvon
1,979 feet (604m)
**Motto**
*Si Quaeris Peninsulam Amoenam Circumspice*
(If You Seek a Pleasant Peninsula, Look About You)
**Song**
"Michigan, my Michigan"

# MINNESOTA

The northernmost state in the United States, apart from Alaska, Minnesota is also known as the North Star State. Car license plates proclaim "10,000 lakes," but in fact there are over 15,000, and the scenic beauty of the state attracts visitors from all over the nation. Minnesota is also one of the Great Lakes states, with its northeastern border on Lake Superior. Here, at the busy port of Duluth, timber, grain, iron ore, and industrial goods are shipped to other states along the 2,342-mile (3,768-km) route, via the lakes and the St. Lawrence Seaway to the Atlantic. In the southeast of the state the twin cities of Minneapolis–St. Paul straddle the Mississippi River and dominate the surrounding region. Minneapolis is one of the most important manufacturing cities in the United States. Among the goods produced are food products and electronic equipment. Grain from the Midwest is stored here, too, before being shipped to other destinations. St. Paul is the state capital. Southern Minnesota is largely prairie land, where farms produce soybeans, corn, and sugar beets. Wheat and other grains contribute to the state's wealth, as does the dairy industry. Other Minnesota products include pulp and paper and iron ore.

French-Canadians were the first settlers in the region. They encountered Native American tribes, including Chippewa and Sioux. The land east of the Mississippi came under U.S. control in 1783, and that to the west was part of the Louisiana Purchase of 1803. Later an influx of Norwegians, Swedes, and Danes settled in Minnesota to work in the mining and timber trades. In the 1900s African-Americans came to work in the factories, followed by Poles, Germans, Hispanics, and Asians.

### BALD EAGLE
Much of northern Minnesota consists of vast tracts of forests sprinkled with clear-blue lakes. Such a wilderness attracts the bald eagle, the national symbol. Although rare, it favors the western Great Lakes region because of its fish diet.

### HIGH-TECH INDUSTRY
Minnesota is a leading state in the computer industry, and some of the world's foremost manufacturers have high-tech plants in Minneapolis–St. Paul. In this picture workers are examining a magnified computer circuit board.

*Pink and white lady's slipper*

*Red (Norway) pine*

### STATE SYMBOLS

*Common loon*

### MINNEAPOLIS
New glass office towers and hotels, tree-lined plazas, fountains, and even enclosed pedestrian skyways (an alternative to the normally frozen winter walkways) all indicate that Minneapolis is a thriving city. Much of its wealth comes from business, including computers, but also from its long-standing milling industries. Household names such as General Mills and Target have their headquarters here.

## MINNESOTA

**Capital**
St. Paul
**Area**
79,610 sq. mi.
(206,174 sq. km)
**Population**
5,197,621 (2007)
**Largest cities**
Minneapolis (369,051)
St. Paul (287,151)
**Statehood**
May 11, 1858
Rank: 32nd
**Principal rivers**
Minnesota
Mississippi
**Highest point**
Eagle Mountain
2,301 feet (702m)
**Motto**
*L'Etoile du Nord*
(The Star of the North)
**Song**
"Hail! Minnesota"

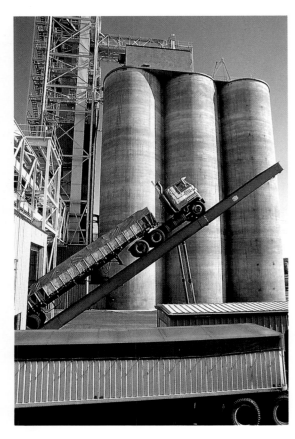

## GRAIN STORAGE STATE

In this dramatic photograph, a grain truck is tilted to empty its load into the elevator. Several of America's—including some of the world's—largest grain and cereal companies are based in Minnesota. Minneapolis has grain storage for over 120 million bushels—the highest in the United States.

## GOPHER STATE

The gopher is a rodent that spends most of its time underground in long tunnels it digs out with its large front claws and teeth. Exactly how this unassuming rodent came to inspire the state's nickname is something of a mystery, although many live in the state.

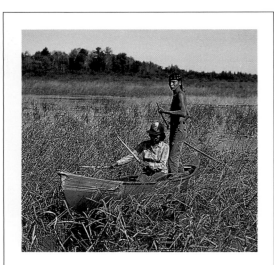

## HARVESTING RICE

Two Native Americans of the Chippewa tribe knock ripe wild rice into their canoe at Leech Lake, in the north of the state. The rice is sold commercially. The Chippewas were among the first tribes in the region, though in prehistoric times Minnesota was inhabited by mound builders. The Chippewas hunted, fished, and gathered wild rice for food. Today they work in many professions. Some live on reservations in Minnesota, North Dakota, and Wisconsin.

## LAKE ITASCA

Lake Itasca is the source of the mighty Mississippi River. It lies in Lake Itasca State Park. Minnesota's thousands of lakes attract canoeists, fishermen, and those who enjoy nature. Animal life includes moose, wolves, beavers, red foxes, and bears. Acres of forest and wildflowers contribute to the state's natural beauty. The rock formations along the lake shores serve as a useful source of information for geologists.

# MISSISSIPPI

A "Deep South" state, Mississippi has 88 miles (142km) of coastline along the Gulf of Mexico between Louisiana and Alabama. The Mississippi River, from which the state takes its name, forms the western border with Louisiana and Arkansas. Along the northern border is Tennessee. Most of the land is flat plains—the highest point in the state is only 806 feet (246m) high—with rich soil for agriculture. The climate is warm and humid in summer, with mild and short winters. Such soil and climate traditionally encouraged a farming economy, with cotton as the main crop. In the pre-Civil War days, slaves worked on huge cotton plantations owned by wealthy whites. These were the antebellum days, when cotton was "king" and white plantation owners enjoyed the spoils of a slave-run economy in their grand balconied mansions. Poorer whites, however, had to compete in a backward rural environment, and many were no better off educationally, socially, or economically than the black slaves. Mississippi became the second state to leave the Union before the Civil War, and Jefferson Davis, himself a Mississippi resident, became President of the Confederate States of America. During the war, from 1861 to 1865, many battles were fought in the state, causing much damage, especially in Vicksburg. After the war the state reverted to being a poor agrarian and racially segregated region. Cotton, along with timber, remained the chief business, and industrialization did not begin until the 1930s with the discovery of oil and the growth of factories turning out textiles, transportation equipment, and electrical goods. The civil rights movement in the 1960s began, finally, to achieve equal rights for African-Americans. Today they account for more than 37 percent of the total state population— higher than any other state.

## STATE SYMBOLS

MEDGAR EVERS
Born in Decatur in 1925, Medgar Evers worked his entire life in civil rights. He campaigned to increase the number of African-American voters. Evers organized boycotts against those who practiced racial discrimination. He was killed by a sniper in 1963.

*Mockingbird*

*Magnolia flower*

*Magnolia tree*

### GRACIOUS HOUSES

Antebellum (pre-Civil War) mansions that belonged to the cotton plantation owners are well preserved in Mississippi, and they attract tourists from all over the country. Natchez, sitting atop a high bluff by the Mississippi River, has many such houses dating from the early- to mid-1800s, including Melrose House shown here. Vicksburg, which saw one of the key battles of the Civil War, also has fine examples. The names of the houses—Auburn, Rosedale, Shadowlawn, Rosalie— recall a sedate, tranquil time, at least for the plantation owners. Life for the slaves was often very harsh.

### COTTON ECONOMY
Cotton plantations, such as the one depicted in this illustration, were the centers of rural life in the Southern states before the Civil War. The cotton itself was the primary source of the South's wealth, and much of this money helped finance the Confederacy at the beginning of the war. This plantation scene looks idyllic, with a paddle steamer gliding down the Mississippi River in the background and the plantation owners in their fine clothes. But life was far from ideal for the slaves, who lived in poverty in slave cabins on the plantations.

## MISSISSIPPI

**Capital**
Jackson
**Area**
48,430 sq. mi.
(125,424 sq. km)
**Population**
2,918,785 (2007)
**Largest cities**
Jackson (175,710)
Gulfport (66,271)
**Statehood**
December 10, 1817
Rank: 20th
**Principal rivers**
Mississippi, Yazoo, Pearl
**Highest point**
Woodall Mountain
806 feet (246m)
**Motto**
*Virtute et Armis*
(By Valor and Arms)
**Song**
"Go, Mississippi!"

### QUEEN OF THE DELTA
The delta is the fertile flood plain between the Mississippi and Yazoo rivers. Here, from the early 1800s on paddle steamers, such as this fine example, the *Mississippi Queen*, transported passengers and goods along the Mississippi River. Today such paddle steamboats carry mainly tourists on the stretch from Natchez to Vicksburg. Forests of hardwood trees and steep bluffs line many parts of the Mississippi River. Along its course the river has cut off areas of land as it meanders, creating small islands.

### CATCHING CATFISH
Three men wade deep to pull in their nets full of Mississippi catfish. These larger versions of the catfish family are also farmed in lakes and streams and are highly prized for their taste. They are bottom-dwellers and use feelers to search for food as they move along. Varieties in the Mississippi River Valley are the channel catfish, the blue catfish, and the yellow catfish. Farther south, at the port of Biloxi, there is a thriving shrimp fleet, which is blessed annually at a special ceremony on the water. Fishing remains an important industry for Mississippi, and catches include menhaden, red snappers, oysters, and carp.

# MISSOURI

Near the geographical center of the continental United States lies the Midwest state of Missouri. It shares borders with eight other states—Arkansas, Iowa, Illinois, Kansas, Kentucky, Nebraska, Oklahoma, and Tennessee. Missouri's history and economy have been shaped by the two great rivers that flow through the state— the Mississippi and the Missouri. The Mississippi forms the eastern border, while the Missouri forms the northwestern border down to Kansas City, where it swings inland across the state. It eventually joins the Mississippi just north of St. Louis.

Missouri is a prosperous state in both agriculture and industry. Its factories make more manufactured goods than all other states, excluding Texas and California. Aircraft, spacecraft, automobiles, leather goods, chemicals, and beer are among the diverse products. Anheuser-Busch, based in St. Louis, is the largest brewery in the world. The contribution to the state economy from manufacturing is worth double that of farming, timber, and mining combined. Livestock, especially cattle, and dairy products are very important, and the chief crops are corn, wheat, soybeans, and cotton. Missouri is the number-one lead producer and second in zinc mining. Lime and cement are also produced. Even when the French first founded Ste. Genevieve, the oldest town in the state, around 1735, lead mining was already established. The United States acquired Missouri from the French in 1803 as part of the Louisiana Purchase. The invention of the steamboat and use of the Mississippi and Missouri rivers as major transportation routes made the state a center of business early in its history. Missouri joined the Union as a slave state in 1821 under the terms of what was called the Missouri Compromise. By this treaty, Maine also became a state—a free state—to keep the number of slave and free states equal. However, Missouri remained loyal to the Union during the Civil War.

**STATE SYMBOLS**

*Bluebird*

*Flowering dogwood*

*Hawthorn*

MARK TWAIN
Author Mark Twain grew up in Hannibal, a town he made famous in *The Adventures of Tom Sawyer* and many other works. The town has a Mark Twain museum, including the two-room cabin, originally located in a nearby settlement, in which he was born as Samuel Clemens in 1835.

OZARK PLATEAU
These springs form part of the Ozark National Park. The Ozark Plateau covers the southern part of Missouri. This region is one of hilly forests and low mountains. It is also an area of thousands of cold and damp caves. Such caves once provided shelter for outlaws such as Jesse James and the Dalton Gang. The Ozark Mountain region is also famous for its special brand of Ozark country music and its chain of lakes that are popular with anglers.

JESSE JAMES
The James gang, led by Jesse James and his brother Frank, staged around 25 violent bank and train robberies in Missouri. Innocent railroad workers were often killed. The famous outlaw was born in Missouri in 1847. He fought on the Southern side during the Civil War with a band of guerillas known as Quantrill's Raiders. After the war James and his gang started their robberies, hiding out from the law in Missouri's many caves. After a reward was offered to catch him dead or alive, James was shot by one of his own gang in 1882.

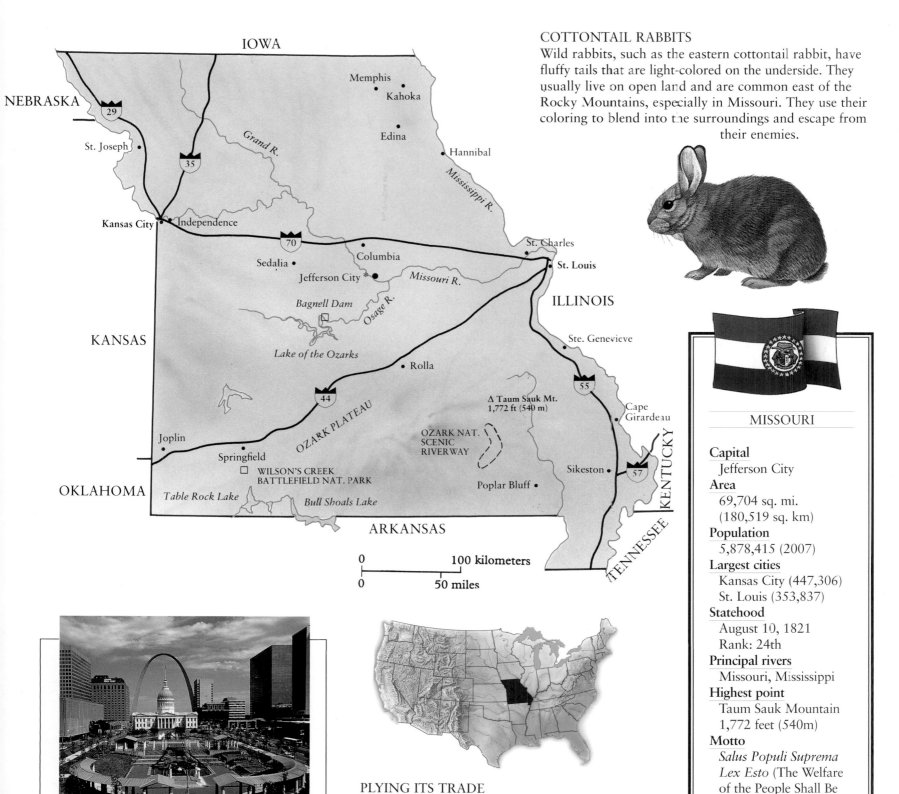

COTTONTAIL RABBITS
Wild rabbits, such as the eastern cottontail rabbit, have fluffy tails that are light-colored on the underside. They usually live on open land and are common east of the Rocky Mountains, especially in Missouri. They use their coloring to blend into the surroundings and escape from their enemies.

## MISSOURI

**Capital**
Jefferson City
**Area**
69,704 sq. mi.
(180,519 sq. km)
**Population**
5,878,415 (2007)
**Largest cities**
Kansas City (447,306)
St. Louis (353,837)
**Statehood**
August 10, 1821
Rank: 24th
**Principal rivers**
Missouri, Mississippi
**Highest point**
Taum Sauk Mountain
1,772 feet (540m)
**Motto**
*Salus Populi Suprema Lex Esto* (The Welfare of the People Shall Be the Supreme Law)
**Song**
"Missouri Waltz"

ST. LOUIS—GATEWAY TO THE WEST
The gleaming curve of Gateway Arch forms a backdrop to the modern skyline of St. Louis. The arch itself is stainless steel and was built in 1965. Its height of 630 feet (192m) is unmatched by any other national monument. The arch commemorates the thousands of pioneers who passed through St. Louis on their way west, and at its base there is a Museum of Westward Expansion. St. Louis is the most important inland port along the Mississippi, and it is 10 miles (16km) south of where the Missouri River meets the Mississippi.

PLYING ITS TRADE
A giant barge carries its cargo on the Mississippi River, which forms Missouri's eastern border. Most freight on the Mississippi is carried in large barges such as this one. Agricultural products, coal, and steel make up most of the cargo.

# MONTANA

Montana is the fourth-largest state in the country but has fewer than one million people—only 6.5 per square mile. The name of this northwestern state comes from the Spanish word for "mountainous," although 75 percent of the land is flat or gently rolling Great Plains. It is in western Montana, lying in the Rocky Mountains, that the land rises to between 6,500 and 13,000 feet (2,000 and 4,000m) above sea level. To the north Montana shares its border with three Canadian provinces—Saskatchewan, Alberta, and British Columbia. In the southwest of the state the Missouri River begins its great journey in the Rocky Mountains and then runs eastward across the state. The Yellowstone River is also an important river in the state. Both rivers supply vitally-needed water to humans, cattle, and crops. Montana has a continental climate, which means that it has very cold winters and hot summers. Until Alaska joined the Union, Montana was the coldest state.

It is on the Plains that vast herds of cattle and sheep—among the largest numbers in the country—graze. Montana is also a producer of barley, wheat, and sugar beets, and there is a large timber industry. But, as its nickname of "Treasure State" suggests, Montana is a land rich in natural minerals, particularly gold, silver, copper, and coal.

The United States acquired most of Montana in the Louisiana Purchase of 1803, and soon after Lewis and Clark explored the region. Fur traders started visiting the area, and the Native American tribes that lived there began to resist the growing influx of white settlers prospecting for gold. The Battle of the Little Bighorn, or Custer's Last Stand, took place in Montana in 1876 between the U.S. cavalry and a coalition of Native American tribes. The opening of the Northern Pacific Railroad in 1883 and a major silver discovery in 1886 near Butte led to more settlers arriving and to the state joining the Union in 1889.

## JEANETTE RANKIN
A social worker and the first woman elected to Congress, Jeanette Rankin was born near Missoula in 1880. A Republican, she represented Montana in Washington from 1916–1918 and again from 1941–1943. She opposed the U.S. entry into World War I, cast the only vote against entering World War II, and later spoke out against participation in the Korean War. She died in 1973.

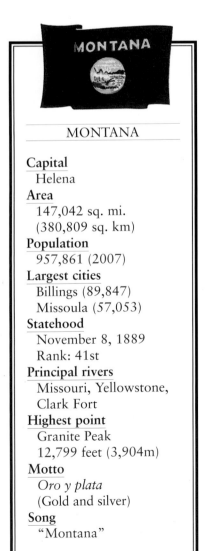

## MONTANA

**Capital**
Helena
**Area**
147,042 sq. mi.
(380,809 sq. km)
**Population**
957,861 (2007)
**Largest cities**
Billings (89,847)
Missoula (57,053)
**Statehood**
November 8, 1889
Rank: 41st
**Principal rivers**
Missouri, Yellowstone,
Clark Fort
**Highest point**
Granite Peak
12,799 feet (3,904m)
**Motto**
Oro y plata
(Gold and silver)
**Song**
"Montana"

STATE SYMBOLS

Ponderosa pine

Western meadowlark

Bitterroot

### BIGHORN CANYON
Spreading across the Montana-Wyoming border, Bighorn Canyon provides spectacular scenic and historic sites. Nearby Yellowtail Dam has created a 71-mile (114-km) reservoir that is popular with anglers and water-sports enthusiasts. Tourism is important to the state's economy, with hunters, fishermen, and campers vacationing in Montana's many parks. The southwest boundary of the state borders Yellowstone National Park, while the northern border with Canada includes Glacier National Park—with over 60 glaciers.

## SCATTERED FARMS

Like islands in a sea of checkered wheatfields, farmhouses stand out on the flat Great Plains of Montana. Immense fields of winter wheat are typical in the eastern part of the state. Agriculture serves as the state's greatest source of income, and Montana ranks in the nation's top ten in the production of wheat and barley. Livestock, particularly cattle, sheep, and pigs, accounts for 50 percent of agricultural income. There are over 2.5 million cattle in the state.

## THE SWIFT PRONGHORN

The pronghorn lives in open grassland, typically on the high Great Plains of Montana. It is one of North America's fastest mammals, and it can travel at speeds of up to 44 miles per hour (70km/h), which enables it to outrun wolves and coyotes. It is often called the American antelope, although it is not a true antelope.

## RODEO SHOW

A cowboy shows his prowess on a bronco at the Big Timber Rodeo. Rodeo is a form of entertainment featuring cowboys and cowgirls who demonstrate their riding and roping skills. It developed from the cowboy cattle-herding days in the western United States from the mid-1860s to the late 1880s. The main events at rodeos are bareback bronco riding, saddle bronco riding, bull riding, calf roping, and steer wrestling (or bulldogging). With a strong cowboy tradition in Montana, it is not surprising that there are many rodeo shows in the state.

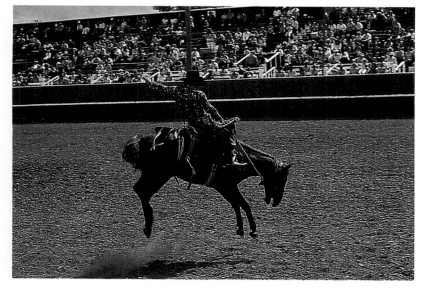

# NEBRASKA

Nebraska, in the heart of the Great Plains, is one of the great farming states of the nation, and its nickname of "Cornhusker State" refers to its most valuable crop. Most of Nebraska is prairie land, but near its western border with Colorado and Wyoming the elevation reaches one mile high. Nebraska has very cold winters and hot summers. Blizzards and windstorms often hit the state, as do droughts. Farmers get their water supply from the Missouri River in the east, which separates the state from Iowa and Missouri, and from the Platte River, which runs west-east across the state. Most industry is related to farming: Omaha, the largest city, is one of the country's leading meat-packing centers. Factories in the state also process grain into breakfast foods. Other manufactured items include machinery, electrical goods, metal products, and transportation equipment. Natural minerals in the state include petroleum and natural gas. Construction industries use large amounts of sand and gravel from the Platte Valley, and limestone is used to make cement. Before the Louisiana Purchase of 1803, the area had been visited by French and Spanish trappers and fur traders in the 1700s. Lewis and Clark also passed through in 1804–1806 on their famous expedition through the Louisiana Territory. The first permanent settlement was in Bellevue, near Omaha, in 1823. The Homestead Act of 1862 encouraged many Civil War veterans to move to Nebraska with the promise of cheap land. Pioneers, prospectors, and cowboys passed through Nebraska following the Oregon Trail or the routes used by the Mormons or by Lewis and Clark. They were helped on their journeys by such land-marks as Chimney Rock and the 800-foot (244-m) high Scotts Bluff on the state's western edge. Pony Express riders also used these landmarks as route guides. Buffalo Bill held his Wild West show in North Platte, and Jesse James and his gang roamed the plains. The transcontinental railroad, which came through in 1863, also helped open up the region. Nebraska is unique in having a one-house state legislature (all other states have an upper and a lower house).

LINCOLN
Founded in 1859, Lincoln was originally named Lancaster but was renamed in honor of the Civil War president, Abraham Lincoln. The Sheldon Art Gallery, which contains some fine paintings, the Folsom Children's Zoo, and the University of Nebraska are located in Lincoln.

STATE SYMBOLS

*Cottonwood*

*Western meadowlark*

*Goldenrod*

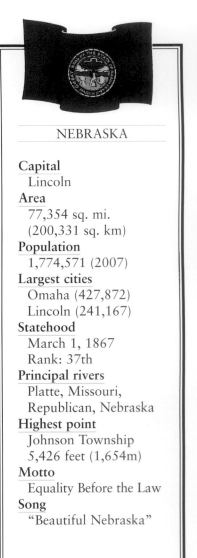

### NEBRASKA

**Capital**
Lincoln
**Area**
77,354 sq. mi.
(200,331 sq. km)
**Population**
1,774,571 (2007)
**Largest cities**
Omaha (427,872)
Lincoln (241,167)
**Statehood**
March 1, 1867
Rank: 37th
**Principal rivers**
Platte, Missouri,
Republican, Nebraska
**Highest point**
Johnson Township
5,426 feet (1,654m)
**Motto**
Equality Before the Law
**Song**
"Beautiful Nebraska"

BUFFALO BILL'S HOME
Near North Platte in the west-central part of Nebraska is Buffalo Bill Ranch State Historical Park. Frontier scout and cowboy-showman William F. "Buffalo Bill" Cody lived in this house while he put together his Wild West rodeos. So popular were his shows that one "Old Glory Blow-Out" held in North Platte in 1872 attracted 1,000 contestants. Bill started a traveling Wild West show, which opened in Omaha in 1883. These shows popularized his and other cowboys' skills across the United States and overseas.

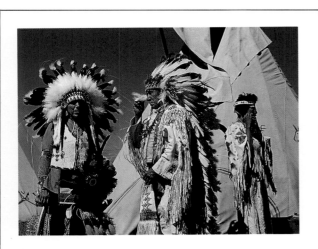

## THE SIOUX

The Sioux are a Great Plains tribe, and Nebraska was one of their hunting grounds (along with Minnesota and South Dakota). During the 1860s and 1870s the Sioux fought against European settlers who were trying to make homesteads in these states. There was constant fighting between the U.S. Army and Sioux warriors led by chiefs Crazy Horse, Red Cloud, and Sitting Bull. The Sioux used their skills as horsemen to outmaneuver the heavily armed and U.S. troops. They were highly effective at the Battle of the Little Bighorn in Montana. These modern day Sioux (above) are dressed in their ceremonial costumes.

## A GREAT FARMING STATE

Nebraska is one of the most important farming states in the nation. It ranks behind only Texas and Iowa in the number of cattle and calves— 6.4 million—raised in the state each year. It also raises over 17 million chickens and almost 3 million hogs. Most of the cattle grazing takes place in the Sand Hills region of western Nebraska, and cowboys patrolling their vast herds in this area are a common sight. The output of its 54,000 farms equals the value of the state's industries, timber, and mining combined. After corn the most valuable crops are hay, oats, wheat, sorghum, soybeans, and sugar beets.

## UNELECTED PRESIDENT

The 38th President of the United States, Gerald R. Ford, was born in Omaha on July 14, 1913. He was the only president not elected to office. He was appointed, not elected, as vice-president, and took over the presidency from Richard Nixon, who resigned in 1973.

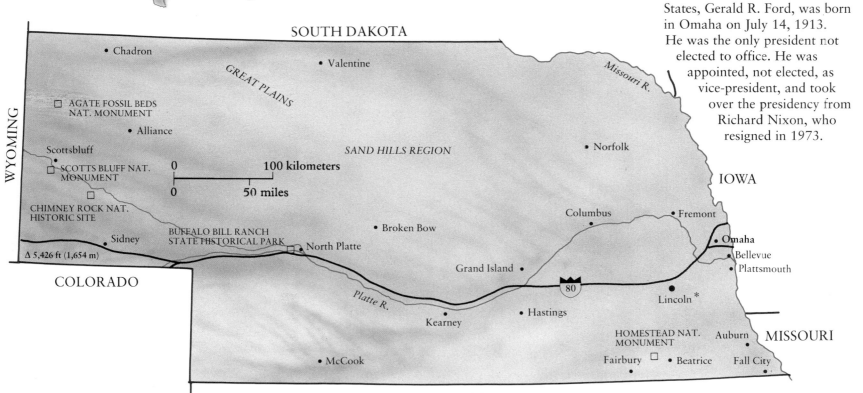

SOUTH DAKOTA

- Chadron
- Valentine

GREAT PLAINS

Missouri R.

AGATE FOSSIL BEDS NAT. MONUMENT

- Alliance

WYOMING

SAND HILLS REGION

- Norfolk

Scottsbluff

SCOTTS BLUFF NAT. MONUMENT

0        100 kilometers

0      50 miles

IOWA

CHIMNEY ROCK NAT. HISTORIC SITE

Columbus
- Fremont

BUFFALO BILL RANCH STATE HISTORICAL PARK

- Broken Bow

△ 5,426 ft (1,654 m)

- Sidney
- North Platte

- Omaha
- Bellevue
- Plattsmouth

COLORADO

Grand Island

80

Platte R.

Lincoln *

- Kearney
- Hastings

HOMESTEAD NAT. MONUMENT

Auburn

MISSOURI

Fairbury ☐ - Beatrice

Fall City

- McCook

KANSAS

# NEVADA

If it were not for the lure of gold, silver, and gambling, Nevada might have remained a vast, mainly uninhabited land of rugged mountains, arid desert, buttes, and mesas. Nevada is the driest and one of the hottest states in the Union. The land receives an average of only 4 inches (10cm) of rain and snow in a year— compared to neighboring Oregon's annual 60 inches (152cm) along its coast. Other states that border this Rocky Mountain state are Idaho to the north; Utah to the east; Arizona at its southern tip across the Colorado River and the famous Hoover Dam; and California to the west. The boundary with California runs at such an angle that Carson City, the state capital, actually lies farther west than Los Angeles. Some 85 percent of the land is owned by the federal government—much of it used to test weapons.

Paiute Native Americans were the first inhabitants, and so unwelcoming was the terrain that it was one of the last parts of the West to be explored—dying of thirst was a real danger for early explorers. Mormons were the first white settlers in this inhospitable terrain; they established the first settlement, Mormon Station (now Genoa), in 1849. The discovery of gold and silver brought thousands of prospectors to establish mining towns, including Virginia City. Many such places are now deserted "ghost towns." Gold and silver remain important sources of income, and Nevada leads all states in the production of these metals.

However, one-third of the jobs in the state come from the gambling and entertainment resorts of Las Vegas and Reno. Tourism is the state's primary source of income, and the main industry is the manufacture of gambling equipment, followed by chemicals, aerospace products, and irrigation equipment. There is some farming in the state, with just over half a million cattle. Alfalfa and potatoes are the main crops. The timber industry produces wood pulp from piñon and juniper trees.

**LAKE TAHOE**
Lying on the Nevada-California border, Lake Tahoe has a 72-mile (116-km) shoreline of public beaches and parks, as well as resorts and gambling casinos. It is the largest mountain lake on the North American continent. The lake lies 6,226 feet (1,899m) above sea level, surrounded by snow-capped mountains.

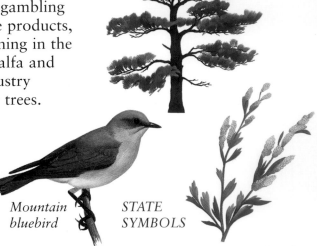

*Single-leaf piñon*

*Mountain bluebird*  **STATE SYMBOLS**

*Sagebrush*

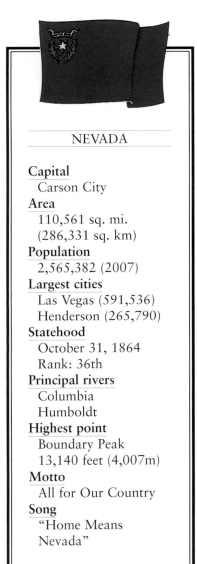

## NEVADA

**Capital**
Carson City
**Area**
110,561 sq. mi.
(286,331 sq. km)
**Population**
2,565,382 (2007)
**Largest cities**
Las Vegas (591,536)
Henderson (265,790)
**Statehood**
October 31, 1864
Rank: 36th
**Principal rivers**
Columbia
Humboldt
**Highest point**
Boundary Peak
13,140 feet (4,007m)
**Motto**
All for Our Country
**Song**
"Home Means Nevada"

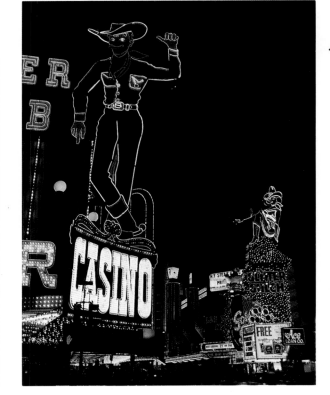

**CITY OF NEON**
Las Vegas beckons tourists, with its giant neon signs, to the many casinos, hotels, entertainment centers—and even to places where you can get instant marriages and instant divorces. Early Native Americans called the Basketmakers inhabited the region from 300 B.C. to A.D. 1150. Spanish explorers came in 1776 and founded Las Vegas, naming it after the Spanish words for "the meadows." Until this century it was a farming community. Gambling was made legal in 1931, and this provided the impetus to develop a city in the middle of nowhere and out of nothing. Las Vegas is now the state's largest city and also boasts the largest resort hotel in the world.

OREGON    IDAHO

SANTA ROSA RANGE

BLACK ROCK DESERT

ISHOSHONE MOUNTAINS

Winnemucca

SMOKE CREEK DESERT

Tungsten

Elko

DIAMOND MOUNTAINS

RUBY MOUNTAINS

Pyramid Lake

GREAT BASIN

Sparks

Reno

Fallon

Virginia City

Carson City *

Ely

Lake Tahoe

GREAT BASIN NAT. PARK    UTAH

Genoa

Walker Lake

Hawthorne

0    100 kilometers

0    50 miles    Caliente

Δ Boundary Peak 13,140 ft (4,007 m)

CALIFORNIA

WHITE MOUNTAINS

CACTUS RANGE

Goldfield    Elgin

DEATH VALLEY NAT. MONUMENT

SHEEP RANGE

SPRING MOUNTAINS

Las Vegas    Lake Mead

Paradise    Henderson

Hoover Dam

Boulder City

Colorado R.    ARIZONA

## BRISTLECONE PINES

North of Death Valley, which runs across the Nevada–California border, stand bristlecone pines. They are high up—13,000 feet (4,000m)—in the White Mountains, and accessible only in summer. They are reputed to be the oldest trees on earth, and some have been dated back over 4,500 years. Probably the oldest one of all, named Methuselah, is almost 4,700 years old. They are twisted by the wind, and their few bristles, or needles, stay on the tree for up to 30 years.

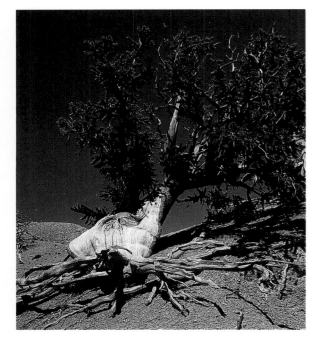

## HOOVER DAM

Now over 60 years old, Hoover Dam (formerly Boulder Dam) stands majestically at the head of the artificial lake it helped create—Lake Mead. The lake provided water and power for the growth of Las Vegas after World War II. The lake extends for 105 miles (170km) behind the dam. It is a popular lake with both fishermen and houseboat renters. Hoover Dam is one of the world's largest hydroelectric plants, and its construction helped the development of the state as a whole by providing water and power.

## RATTLESNAKES

Among the most poisonous of snakes, rattlesnakes live in dry western regions, such as Nevada's deserts. The snake often gives a warning by lifting its tail and shaking the rattle on its end before it strikes. Its venom is injected by its sharp fangs and can quickly paralyze, and eventually kill, its prey.

# NEW HAMPSHIRE

Located in the northeastern corner of the United States, New Hampshire is the third-largest of the six New England states. It was the first colony to declare independence from England, and every four years it is the first state to hold U.S. presidential primary elections. This makes the state the focus of media attention as the candidates come to national prominence—for many of them it is the first and only time. Only two candidates in recent history have lost this primary and gone on to become presidents.

New Hampshire has a narrow 18-mile (29-km) stretch of Atlantic coastline, and its greatest width is only a little over 90 miles (150km). From north to south it measures 180 miles (290km) but narrows to a northern border with Canada of just 15 miles (24km) across. In the north are the White Mountains, which have rock outcroppings that have given New Hampshire its nickname of the "Granite State." Mount Washington, the highest peak in the Northeast at 6,288 feet (1,917m), is also located there. This peak is one of the windiest places on the planet; the highest known wind speeds have been recorded there. New Hampshire suffered a devastating blow in May 2003, when its most famous landmark, a 40-foot (12-m)-high rock formation called the Old Man of the Mountains, also known as the Great Stone Face, fell off. The Connecticut River runs along most of the state's western border with Vermont. Over 80 percent of the land is covered by forest—white pine, hemlock, oak, and birch—which yields lumber, wood pulp, and paper products. Most of New Hampshire's people and industries are in the southern part of the state. Tourism and forestry are the major industries, followed by the manufacture of machinery, electrical products, plastics, and metal products. The four largest cities are all located in this region, and all once had textile mills. Many of the newer manufacturers have moved there from the nearby Boston area because New Hampshire has lower taxes.

The first known Native Americans in New Hampshire, the Abnaki tribe, were driven out by English settlers, who settled there in 1623. In the 1800s New Hampshire was noted for its textile mills, and many French-Canadians came to work these mills at that time. Today there are still more French-Canadians in New Hampshire than in any other state.

*White birch*

**STATE SYMBOLS**

*Purple finch*

*Purple lilac*

## NEW HAMPSHIRE

**Capital**
Concord
**Area**
9,350 sq. mi.
(24,215 sq. km)
**Population**
1,315,828 (2007)
**Largest cities**
Manchester (107,219)
Nashua (87,285)
Concord (41,823)
**Statehood**
June 21, 1788
Rank: 9th
**Principal rivers**
Connecticut
Merrimack
Androscoggin
**Highest point**
Mt. Washington
6,288 feet (1,917m)
**Motto**
Live Free or Die
**Song**
"Old New Hampshire"

### FRANKLIN PIERCE
The 14th president of the United States, Franklin Pierce, was born in New Hampshire and served in the New Hampshire legislature from 1829 to 1833. He was elected president in 1852, at a time when conflict between North and South over slavery was deepening. He was a compromise candidate who was trusted by the South, even though he was a Northerner.

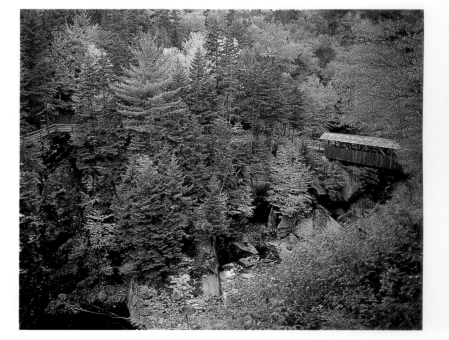

### RURAL MOUNTAIN LAND
A covered wooden pedestrian bridge spans a thickly wooded river valley in Franconia Notch State Park in New Hampshire. Notches are long wooded gaps, or deep valleys, and land forms that separate the mountains. Franconia Notch is a famous landmark in the state. Another is Profile Mountain, which bears the rock formation known as the Great Stone Face. The White Mountains, in which these landmarks are located, cover the northern third of the state.

## PORTSMOUTH

Lying at the north of New Hampshire's short stretch of Atlantic coastline, Portsmouth is one of the state's largest cities, with a population of around 21,000. The port developed during the Industrial Revolution of the 1800s, with its textile mills, woodworking, shoemaking, and clothing manufacture. In the 1950s the textile mills gave way to factories and other firms developing high technology.

## MARY BAKER EDDY

Mary Baker Eddy was the founder of the Christian Science religion. She was born in New Hampshire in 1821 and suffered from poor health. Her experience with a faith healer led her to conclude that the practice of medicine was not the true means of treating illness. Eventually she came to believe that healing could only begin when a patient had faith in God. In 1879 she established the First Church of Christ, Scientist and in 1908 founded the *Christian Science Monitor* newspaper. She died in 1910.

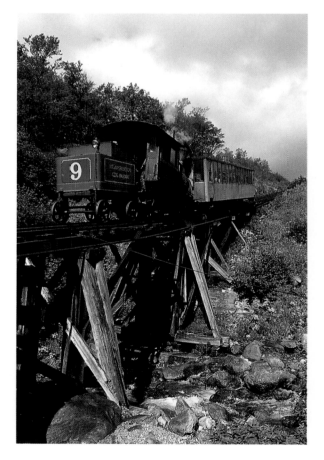

## MT. WASHINGTON RAILWAY

This famous cog railway takes vacationers to the 6,288-foot (1,917-m) summit of New Hampshire's highest mountain. The 3.5-mile (5.5-km) line has been in operation since the 1860s. It offers superb views of the surrounding tree-covered White Mountains. A network of trails spread out from Mt. Washington, attracting hikers, campers, skiers, fishermen, and hunters.

# NEW JERSEY

A small state in area, New Jersey is hemmed in between two of the largest urban complexes in the United States—New York City and Philadelphia. Many people drive through or commute between these cities, hardly seeing New Jersey at all. However, they are missing a state of surprising variety. It is surrounded by water on all sides except for the 50-mile (80-km) border with New York to the north. New Jersey has a stretch of Atlantic coastline that runs for 130 miles (209km). To the northeast are the Hudson River and Lower New York Bay. The Delaware River serves as the state's western border with Pennsylvania, flowing south into Delaware Bay.

Farms in the central and southwestern parts of the state give New Jersey its nickname of "Garden State"—a somewhat surprising title, as the entire population is classified as living in metropolitan areas. But market gardening is a major business, and the land has rich soil, ideal for growing crops such as potatoes, peaches, cranberries, and blueberries, as well as tomatoes, corn, hay, and soybeans. New Jersey ranks in the top ten for manufacturing; among its products are pharmaceutical drugs, chemicals, and petroleum products. The state has witnessed many famous scientific inventions, including Thomas Edison's invention of the electric light and the phonograph. Edison set up the nation's first research laboratory in New Jersey in 1876.

A thriving fishing industry brings in catches of menhaden, clams, and swordfish. The first residents in the state were Delaware Native Americans, and the first Native American Reservation in the country was set up for them in 1758 by the English settlers who had arrived there in 1664. The English took over from earlier Dutch and Swedish settlers.

*Eastern goldfinch*

*Purple violet*

STATE SYMBOLS

*Red oak*

ON THE BOARDWALK
Atlantic City is a well-known resort town on the southeast coast of New Jersey, and is especially famous for its 4.5-mile (7.2-km) boardwalk. The first boardwalk was built in 1870 and was only 8 feet (2m) wide. The modern version has amusement piers that jut out from it, adding to the carnival atmosphere with vendors, exhibits, shows, and food outlets. Gambling is also legal.

THE DELWARE RIVER
The Delaware River, with its many tree-covered banks and islands, forms New Jersey's western border with Pennsylvania. River valleys such as this one produce oak, elm, birch, ash, and maple trees.

A STADIUM FOR GIANTS
The Meadowlands, only a few miles from New York City, offers a unique sports and entertainment stadium. It opened in East Rutherford in 1976 and remains one of the most modern sports complexes in the world. Both the New York Giants and the New York Jets professional football teams play there. Other attractions at the stadium include basketball and harness racing.

## COUNT BASIE
William Basie was born in Red Bank in 1904. His life was devoted to music, and he was dubbed "Count" while working as a young disc jockey. He went on to become a jazz composer and bandleader. He eventually turned from solo playing to musical arrangement. He died in 1984.

## OPOSSUM
Opossum are most common in the central and eastern parts of the country, such as New Jersey. They have more teeth than any other North American mammal —50 in all—and use their long tails to hang from tree branches.

## BATSTO MILL
This gristmill—a mill for grinding grain into flour—is found in Batsto, a partially restored village in southeastern New Jersey that dates back to colonial times. The community produced cannonballs for George Washington's troops during the Revolutionary War. Other attractions in the village include a blacksmith's shop, a general store, and a glassware exhibition.

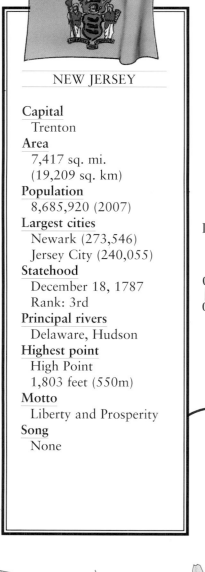

## NEW JERSEY

**Capital**
Trenton
**Area**
7,417 sq. mi.
(19,209 sq. km)
**Population**
8,685,920 (2007)
**Largest cities**
Newark (273,546)
Jersey City (240,055)
**Statehood**
December 18, 1787
Rank: 3rd
**Principal rivers**
Delaware, Hudson
**Highest point**
High Point
1,803 feet (550m)
**Motto**
Liberty and Prosperity
**Song**
None

## PRINCETON UNIVERSITY
Students sit outside the attractive Princeton clock tower of this famous university, founded in 1746. It is one of the oldest and finest universities in the country. The campus is in the town of Princeton itself. The great physicist Albert Einstein worked there when he first arrived in the United States. The town of Princeton is also home of Princeton Battlefield, scene of a decisive American victory in 1777 by General George Washington in the Revolutionary War.

# NEW MEXICO

A land of beautiful deserts, mesas, mountains, canyons, caves, and buttes, New Mexico is justly named the "Land of Enchantment." Its history goes back thousands of years and embraces several different cultures: those of cliff-dwelling Native Americans, whose ancient pueblos can still be seen and whose descendants live there today; of Spanish colonists, who established a capital in Santa Fe in 1609 (about the same time as the first British settlements on the Atlantic coast); of Mexicans, who owned the territory between 1821 and 1848; and finally of white Americans, who began moving into the territory in the mid-1800s. In 1945 New Mexico came to the world's attention as the site of the first testing of the atomic bomb.

The Rocky Mountains enter the state along its northern border with Colorado. Arizona is to the west and to the south lie Mexico and part of Texas, which also takes up most of the eastern border. New Mexico has very little surface water—less than any other state—so irrigation for both livestock and crops is vital. Crops include cotton, hay, onions, wheat, pecans, and sorghum. Much of the land is grazed by cattle and sheep. Most of the state's wealth comes from minerals—oil and natural gas. New Mexico is the leading state in the mining of potash and uranium. Copper, silver, iron, and lead are also mined.

It was the prospect of silver and gold that first lured the Spanish explorer Francisco Coronado to the area in 1540 and that led to the forming of a colony in 1598. The same metals brought another wave of settlers to work the mines in the 1800s. When Mexico gained independence from Spain in 1821, New Mexico became part of that country. Following the Mexican War of 1846–1848, the territory was acquired by the United States, but it was disputed until 1912 when New Mexico became a state. The state has one of the largest Mexican and Hispanic-American populations in the United States.

CHURCHES MADE OF MUD
San Geronimo Church in Taos displays the typical pueblo architecture of adobe walls, enclosed patios, buttressed corners, and portals. New Mexico's generally dry and sunny climate has ensured the survival of such buildings for centuries. In 1671 Spanish settlers discovered a Native American Pueblo that had existed in Taos from around A.D. 1000. There was much trade of grain, pottery, and jewelry between the Spanish, Pueblos, and other Native Americans who traveled from across the mountains.

*Yucca*

*Piñon*

STATE SYMBOLS

*Roadrunner*

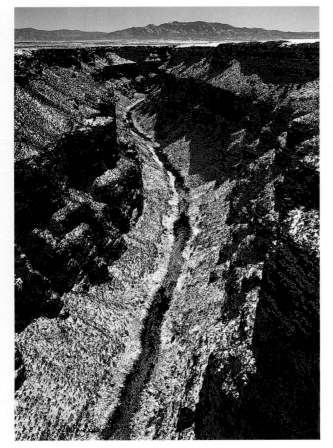

RIO GRANDE
Near the Spanish-Native American village of Taos lies the spectacular Rio Grande Gorge, carved by the Rio Grande over thousands of years. The elevation of the gorge is 2,500 feet (763m), and it is often covered with snow in winter, creating breathtaking views. The Rio Grande begins in southern Colorado and flows south for over 1,885 miles (3,034km), making it one of the longest rivers in North America.

## NEW MEXICO

**Capital**
Santa Fe
**Area**
121,589 sq. mi.
(314,891 sq. km)
**Population**
1,969,915 (2007)
**Largest cities**
Albuquerque (518,271)
Las Cruces (89,722)
**Statehood**
January 6, 1912
Rank: 47th
**Principal rivers**
Rio Grande, Canadian,
Pecos
**Highest point**
Wheeler Peak
13,161 feet (4,014m)
**Motto**
*Crescit Eundo*
(It Grows As It Goes)
**Song**
"O, Fair New Mexico"

## HOPI SUN GOD

Hopi kachinas (spirit followers) wear colorful face masks representing a variety of gods, spirits, and clouds, including the sun god, Tawa Kachina, shown here. The Hopi are the most western group of Pueblo Native Americans. Most live in northeastern Arizona, but some make their home along New Mexico's border with Arizona. Most of them are farmers and shepherds.

## TRACKING THE STARS

The Very Large Array radio telescope contains 27 radio dishes spread over 13 miles (21km) to the north of White Sands Missile Range, where military missiles are tested. New Mexico is a state in which nature's destructive—as well as beneficial—forces have been exploited. Many people in the state are employed in atomic, space, military, and other scientific research, and this contributes to the economy. It was on July 16, 1945, that the world's first atomic bomb was tested just north of Alamogordo. Within a month two other bombs were dropped on Hiroshima and Nagasaki in Japan, ending World War II.

*Teddybear cholla*

*Claret cup cactus*

*Beavertail cactus*

*Cushion cactus*

*Peyote*

## DESERT BLOOD

Desert flowers blooming overnight after a sudden thunderstorm are reminders that New Mexico is indeed a state of enchantment. Cacti survive the dry climate of New Mexico by storing up large amounts of water in their stems. The thick, waxy skin keeps the water in instead of allowing it to evaporate as in other plants. The sharp needles protect the plants against animals and birds. For a very brief period every year the cacti produce stunning white, red, pink, and yellow flowers. These in turn attract many insects, including butterflies.

# NEW YORK

The third most populous state in the country, New York falls into two distinct parts: New York City—whose metropolitan area extends into New Jersey and Connecticut—and "upstate" New York. New York lies in the Northeast, with many natural boundaries, including Lake Ontario, Lake Erie, Lake Champlain, the Niagara River and Falls, the Atlantic Ocean, and the St. Lawrence and Hudson rivers. Ships ply the St. Lawrence Seaway and the extensive canal system, linking the state to the Midwest and to Canada.

The state has varied and beautiful countryside. To the north lie the Adirondack Mountains, with peaks over 5,000 feet (1,500m) high. The large Allegheny Plateau has much farmland devoted to fruit and dairy products. It also includes the aptly named Finger Lakes. The plateau almost completely surrounds the Catskill Mountains, with their many lakes and resorts. New York's climate is continental, which brings hot summers and cold, snowy winters. In the summer people flock to the beaches, especially those on Long Island. Long Island extends east from the mouth of the Hudson River for about 120 miles (193km). Other key attractions include the spectacular Niagara Falls, the Thousand Islands (where the St. Lawrence River meets Lake Ontario, most of which is in Canada), and of course Manhattan, the center of New York City. The city contains the famous Empire State Building (named for the state itself), the Statue of Liberty, and many other famous sights, and is the nerve center of the nation's banking, finance, trade, communication, publishing, arts, and fashion industries. Tourists come from all over the world to enjoy its concert halls museums, art galleries, theaters, clubs, and restaurants.

The Italian navigator Giovanni da Verrazano (after whom a bridge linking Staten Island to Brooklyn in New York City is named) first visited the region in 1524. The Dutch established a settlement there in 1621, and in 1625 Governor Peter Minuit purchased Manhattan Island from local Native Americans for $24 worth of trinkets. The British took control in 1664 and named it New York after the Duke of York, later King James II of England.

*Sugar maple*

STATE SYMBOLS

*Rose*

*Bluebird*

LADY WITH THE TORCH
The Statue of Liberty, on Liberty Island in New York Harbor, was erected in 1883. It was a gift from France, and it became the first landmark sighted by poor and oppressed immigrants coming in by ship across the Atlantic—a symbol of their entry into a new and free land. The framework is iron, and it is covered in copper. The lady stands 151 feet (46m) tall on a pedestal 154 feet (47m) high.

ADIRONDACK COUNTRYSIDE
Fall colors surround the Black River in the Adirondack Mountains in northeastern New York. The 100 or so mountains that make up the Adirondack range include New York State's highest, Mt. Marcy, at 5,344 feet (1,630m). Over 200 lakes, including long Lake George, lie within this mountain region, which covers 5,000 sq. miles (13,000 sq. km). Sadly there is evidence of acid rain on many lakes. The Adirondacks are covered with spruce, hemlock, and pine forests and were named by Samuel de Champlain in 1609 after a local tribe.

NEW DEAL PRESIDENT
Franklin Delano Roosevelt was born in New York on January 30, 1882, and became the 32nd U.S. President in 1933. The economic Depression was at its worst, but his "New Deal" presidency overhauled the banking system, gave aid to farmers, and financed many public projects. He was helped with many of his duties by his wife Eleanor.

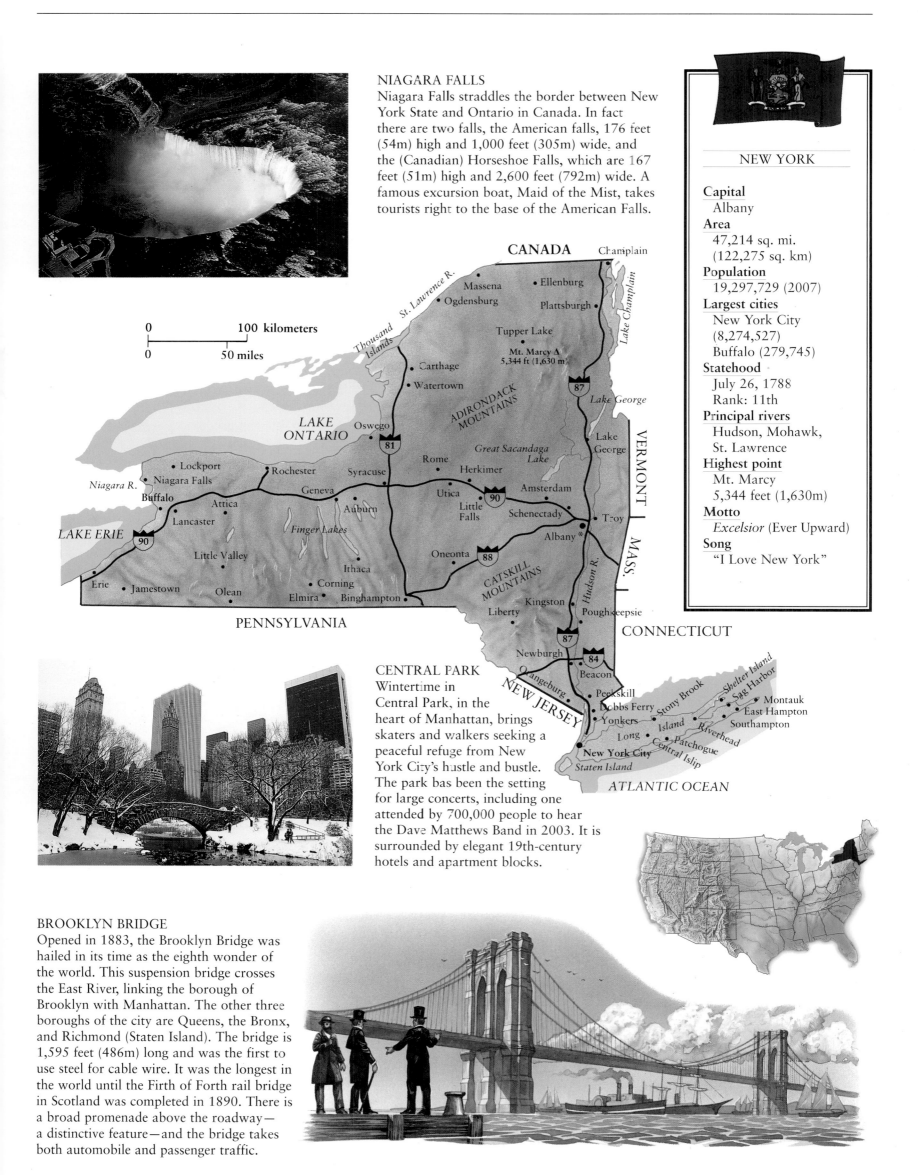

## NIAGARA FALLS

Niagara Falls straddles the border between New York State and Ontario in Canada. In fact there are two falls, the American falls, 176 feet (54m) high and 1,000 feet (305m) wide, and the (Canadian) Horseshoe Falls, which are 167 feet (51m) high and 2,600 feet (792m) wide. A famous excursion boat, Maid of the Mist, takes tourists right to the base of the American Falls.

### NEW YORK

**Capital**
Albany
**Area**
47,214 sq. mi.
(122,275 sq. km)
**Population**
19,297,729 (2007)
**Largest cities**
New York City
(8,274,527)
Buffalo (279,745)
**Statehood**
July 26, 1788
Rank: 11th
**Principal rivers**
Hudson, Mohawk,
St. Lawrence
**Highest point**
Mt. Marcy
5,344 feet (1,630m)
**Motto**
*Excelsior* (Ever Upward)
**Song**
"I Love New York"

## CENTRAL PARK

Wintertime in Central Park, in the heart of Manhattan, brings skaters and walkers seeking a peaceful refuge from New York City's hustle and bustle. The park has been the setting for large concerts, including one attended by 700,000 people to hear the Dave Matthews Band in 2003. It is surrounded by elegant 19th-century hotels and apartment blocks.

## BROOKLYN BRIDGE

Opened in 1883, the Brooklyn Bridge was hailed in its time as the eighth wonder of the world. This suspension bridge crosses the East River, linking the borough of Brooklyn with Manhattan. The other three boroughs of the city are Queens, the Bronx, and Richmond (Staten Island). The bridge is 1,595 feet (486m) long and was the first to use steel for cable wire. It was the longest in the world until the Firth of Forth rail bridge in Scotland was completed in 1890. There is a broad promenade above the roadway— a distinctive feature—and the bridge takes both automobile and passenger traffic.

# NORTH CAROLINA

The southern state of North Carolina has a long history and a richly-varied landscape. Its coastline includes many inlets and islands—one of them the site of the first English colony in North America—enclosed by a long chain of sandbars called the Outer Banks. The shifting sands of these banks are notoriously dangerous for ships, hundreds of which have foundered on them—especially off Cape Hatteras, "Graveyard of the Atlantic." Also on the Outer Banks is Kitty Hawk, where the Wright brothers ushered in the age of powered flight. West of the islands is the coastal plain. The average elevation here is less than 20 feet (6m). Tobacco, North Carolina's most important crop, is grown here. Much of the early work was done by slaves from Africa who were freed after the Civil War. Other crops include soybeans, corn, and peanuts. Farther west is the Piedmont, a rolling plateau that contains the state's chief population and industrial centers. Charlotte, the largest city, is located here. Despite being a rural state, North Carolina leads all states in textiles and furniture production. In fact it is one of the leading industrial states in the nation. High technology products are made in Research Triangle Park, a research center founded in 1959 by three universities. The Piedmont also has most of the state's thriving poultry raising industry. West of the Piedmont the land rises to the Blue Ridge Mountains, and beyond that are the higher Great Smoky Mountains—the highest mountains in the eastern half of the nation. Roanoke Island, inside the Outer Banks, is the site where between 1585 and 1591 the British attempted to establish their first colony in North America. In 1587 Sir Walter Raleigh sent 117 colonists under Governor John White to settle there. Relations with Native Americans were difficult, and the colonists received little help from their sponsors in England. When a ship bearing fresh supplies finally arrived in 1591, the whole colony had vanished. To this day no one knows what happened to the "Lost Colony." But before they disappeared they baptized the first child born of English parents in the New World, White's granddaughter, Virginia Dare. The first permanent settlement was established later in 1653.

*STATE SYMBOLS*

*Longleaf pine*

*Cardinal*

*Flowering dogwood*

**TOBACCO**
Clusters of star-shaped blossoms identify the tobacco plant. North Carolina produces about two-fifths of the U.S. output. Native Americans smoked tobacco as a sacred herb before the first colonists began growing it.

**THE FIRST FLIGHT**
A memorial atop a sand dune commemorates the point from which Orville and Wilbur Wright successfully accomplished the first sustained flight in a craft heavier than air. On December 17, 1903, their "Flyer I" took off from Kitty Hawk. The flight lasted 12 seconds, and that was enough to signal the age of the airplane. Only a few people witnessed this historic event. Orville piloted the first short flight. His brother made a second, longer flight, lasting nearly a minute. In 1908 Orville made a one-hour flight. The original planes are now in the National Air and Space Museum in Washington, D.C.

**BLUE RIDGE MOUNTAINS**
The Blue Ridge Mountains are the major range in North Carolina. The mountain region covers some 6,000 sq. mi. (15,539 sq. km). The temperatures here are cool, and the land is covered mainly with hardwood forests. South of the range is the Piedmont plateau, half of which is covered with timber. It also contains the state's cities and industry.

## NORTH CAROLINA

**Capital**
Raleigh
**Area**
53,819 sq. mi.
(139,380 sq. km)
**Population**
9,061,032 (2007)
**Largest cities**
Charlotte (695,995)
Raleigh (380,173)
**Statehood**
November 21, 1789
Rank: 12th
**Principal rivers**
Roanoke, Yadkin,
Neuse
**Highest point**
Mt. Mitchell
6,684 feet (2,038m)
**Motto**
*Esse Quam Videri* (To
Be Rather Than to Seem)
**Song**
"The Old North State"

### CHARLOTTE
Charlotte, the state's largest city, is one of the fastest growing towns in the nation. It is a center for textiles, machinery, metal, and food processing. It was settled in about 1750, and named after Queen Charlotte, wife of George III of England. In the early 1800s a gold mint was located there, and it was the center of U.S. gold production until the Gold Rush of 1849. During the Civil War it was an important Confederate naval yard. Presidents Andrew Jackson and James Polk were both born nearby and educated in the city.

### BLACK BEAR
The black bear is a good climber and lives in forests all over the United States. So North Carolina, with its large areas of forest-covered land, is an ideal environment for this mammal. Bears are the largest meat-eating animals (carnivores) on the continent, and the smallest of them—the black bear—is the most common species.

### JESSE JACKSON
Born in South Carolina in 1941, Jesse Jackson is one of the great modern civil rights leaders and a potent force in American politics. He lived and went to college in North Carolina and then attended the Chicago Theological Seminary. He worked for the Southern Christian Leadership Conference, where he opened employment opportunities for African-Americans. He later used this experience to expand educational prospects. In the 1980s Jackson worked to secure the release of several political prisoners and hostages. He was a nonvoting member of the Senate from 1990 to 1997, representing the interests of Washington, D.C. Since that time, Jackson has remained heavily involved in civil rights and promoting peace, both nationally and internationally.

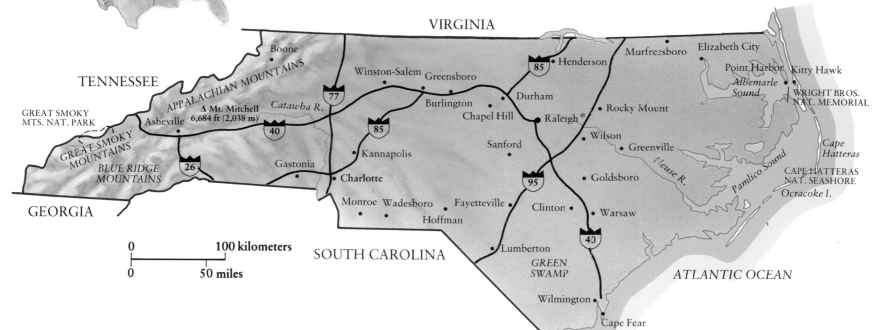

# NORTH DAKOTA

The Great Plains state of North Dakota lies at the center of continental North America. In fact the geographical center is in Pierce County, 6 miles (10km) west of Balta, at latitude 48° 10' N, longitude 100° 10' W. North Dakota's economy is based heavily on farming; the land consisting typically of enormous farms on treeless prairies. The climate is extreme in the state, with summer temperatures reaching as high as 120° F (50°C), and bitterly cold winters falling as low as –60° F (–50°C). The sharp contrasts in climate and the nature of the land may account for the small population of North Dakota— the third-smallest in the United States.

The state rises slowly from the prairie of the east to the high plateau of the west. The Red River forms its eastern border. The Missouri River enters from the west and runs through the center of the state. Eastern North Dakota is especially good for farming, despite a short growing season with little rain. The average farm is an enormous 1,000 acres (405 hectares) in size. The state has substantial deposits of oil and coal but has the least manufacturing of any state. Farm machinery and food products are the main manufactured items.

The western part of the state is too dry for crops, but beef cattle graze there on pastureland. The so-called Badlands are located here, consisting of strange land formations and contours formed by the erosion of soft rock. Directly on the North Dakota border between Canada and the United States lies the International Peace Garden. The land was donated by the two countries as a tribute to over 150 years of peaceful relations.

The first Europeans to visit North Dakota were French fur trappers and traders traveling from Canada in the 1700s. Sioux Native Americans were already established there, and "Dakota" means an alliance of Sioux tribes. Bad relations with the Sioux hindered early white settlement, but the first railroad in the 1870s attracted many more settlers.

**BADLANDS**
Strange rock formations, the result of millions of years of erosion by wind and water, dominate the skyline in North Dakota's Badlands in the southwest. Tablelike mesas and buttes—steep hills standing alone on the plain—are the result of major erosion caused by a large, fast-flowing river that dried up millions of years ago. The name "Badlands" was given to the region by pioneers who found the land difficult to cross. White Butte, situated in the Badlands, is the highest point in the state.

## NORTH DAKOTA

**Capital**
Bismarck
**Area**
70,700 sq. mi.
(183,099 sq. km)
**Population**
639,715 (2007)
**Largest cities**
Fargo (100,000)
Bismarck (58,333)
**Statehood**
November 2, 1889
Rank: 39th
**Principal rivers**
Missouri, Sheyenne,
Little Missouri
**Highest point**
White Butte
3,506 feet (1,069m)
**Motto**
Liberty and Union,
Now and Forever,
One and Inseparable
**Song**
"North Dakota Hymn"

**ROOSEVELT NATIONAL MEMORIAL PARK**
In 1884, Theodore Roosevelt retired temporarily from politics and came to North Dakota to hunt buffalo. He stayed to start up two ranches in Elkhorn and Maltese Cross. The Roosevelt National Memorial Park, one of more than 40 in the state, is a wilderness with coyotes, Rocky Mountain sheep, and buffalo amid buttes and hills.

*STATE SYMBOLS*

*American elm*

*Wild prairie rose*

*Western meadowlark*

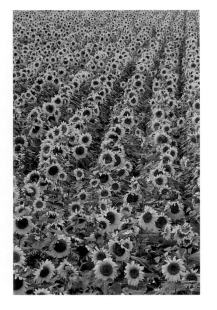

### SUNFLOWERS
The common sunflower is cultivated in North Dakota for its oil, which is used as cooking or salad oil. The remainder of the seed can be made into cattle-cake and food for poultry. Sunflowers can grow as tall as 13 feet (4m).

### A WHEAT STATE
A typical view of North Dakota's farming-dominated land, where giant grain elevators dot the horizon beyond bales of hay ready for collection. Over 90 percent of the land is cropland or pasture. Agriculture far exceeds manufacturing in the state. Wheat is the chief crop; North Dakota is second only to Kansas in wheat production. Other important crops are barley, rye, and oats. Durum wheat, used in making pasta, is grown in the driest areas, where it is particularly suited to the soil and climate. Beef and dairy cattle are also raised in North Dakota. The richest farmlands are in the Red River Valley and on the Great Plains, which stretch from the northwest to the south-central part of the state. North Dakota is the chief flax-growing state.

### WATERFOWL
Every summer ducks, such as gadwalls and mallards, and geese migrate to North Dakota to breed in the lakes, marshes, and grain fields. More waterfowl hatch in North Dakota than in any other state. Another animal native to the state is the flickertail squirrel, from which the state gets one of its nicknames.

*Gadwall* *female*

*male*

*Mallard*

*male*

*female*

### SACAGAWEA
When Meriwether Lewis and William Clark set out to explore the lands bought by the United States in the Louisiana Purchase of 1803, they had a Shoshone Native American woman guide them west. Her name was Sacagawea, which means "Bird Woman," and she was from North Dakota. She was married to a French-Canadian trapper, who acted as an interpreter. Carrying her baby on her back, Sacagawea was influential in appeasing potentially hostile Native American tribes with messages of peace.

# OHIO

Ohio lies at the eastern edge of the Midwestern region. It has more industries and is more urban than almost any other state. The basis of its economy has traditionally come from what are called "smokestack industries," such as steel mills, automobile factories, tires and other rubber products, as well as petroleum, plastics, and chemicals. Several of these industries were set up in the 1850s and 1860s. Ohio is also an important agricultural state, and in the 1850s ranked first in farming. Despite its heavy industrial base, Ohio still has 60 percent of its land given over to farming. The chief crops are corn, hay, and winter wheat, but tobacco is grown in the south, and there are fruit farms along the banks of the Ohio River. Much of the corn is fed to cattle raised in the state.

Some of Ohio's farmers belong to the Amish sect, who still practice a mainly non-mechanized form of farming. They have lived in the state since the 1800s. The eastern part of the state is the most industrialized, but the major cities are fairly well scattered out—from Cleveland in the northeast to Columbus in the center of the state and Cincinnati in the southwest corner. Dayton, also in the west, is an aviation center, with the Wright–Patterson Air Force Base located nearby. The Wright Brothers first experimented with kites, gliders, and flying machines at this field. The U.S. Air Force Museum, at the base, is one of the largest in the world. The first cash register was also made in Dayton by an inventor named James Ritty. Akron, in the northeast, is an important center for rubber manufacturing; some of the most famous tire companies in the world are based there. The first rubber plant was started in Akron in 1879, and the arrival of the automobile toward the end of the century created an enormous demand for pneumatic tires. Columbus, the capital, is the fastest-growing city in the state. Its limestone state capitol building remains one of the finest examples of Greek Revival architecture. Presidents who were born or lived at some time in Ohio include William McKinley, Rutherford B. Hayes, William Henry Harrison, Benjamin Harrison, Ulysses S. Grant, James A. Garfield, and William Howard Taft.

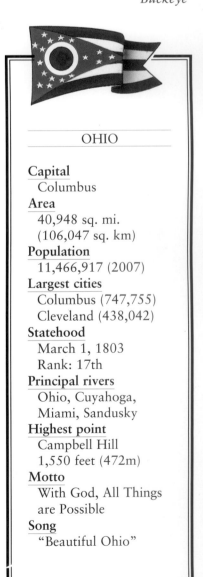

*Cardinal*

**STATE SYMBOLS**

*Scarlet carnation*

*Buckeye*

OHIO

**Capital**
Columbus
**Area**
40,948 sq. mi.
(106,047 sq. km)
**Population**
11,466,917 (2007)
**Largest cities**
Columbus (747,755)
Cleveland (438,042)
**Statehood**
March 1, 1803
Rank: 17th
**Principal rivers**
Ohio, Cuyahoga,
Miami, Sandusky
**Highest point**
Campbell Hill
1,550 feet (472m)
**Motto**
With God, All Things
are Possible
**Song**
"Beautiful Ohio"

### CLEVELAND
Cleveland stands at the mouth of the Cuyahoga River on Lake Erie. It was founded by Moses Cleveland in 1796, when Ohio was part of the Northwest Territory. The city suffered a severe debt problem in the 1970s, but it has come back as a busy commercial center with improved streets and bridges. The city is also a center for the arts with the world-famous Cleveland Orchestra, the Cleveland Museum of Art, and the Natural History Museum.

### ANNIE OAKLEY
Annie Oakley was an expert markswoman and entertainer. She was born in Ohio in 1860 as Phoebe Ann Moses, and typified the spirited, independent women of the American West. The model of "Annie Get Your Gun," she learned to shoot as a child to provide food after her father died. She joined Buffalo Bill's Wild West show in 1885 as the "Peerless Lady Wing-Shot." Oakley instructed soldiers during World War I. She died in 1926.

## CINCINNATI
A nighttime river scene in Cincinnati. The city is located on the north side of the the Ohio River and is the home of the Taft family, including the 27th U.S. President, William Howard Taft. Cincinnati has a big meat industry, linked to transportation on the Ohio River.

## BURIAL MOUNDS
Serpent Mound near Hillsboro is shaped like a giant snake. These burial mounds were built by some of Ohio's earliest inhabitants. They put well-crafted items, such as copper breastplates, tools, shells, carved pipes, and ornaments made of grizzly bear teeth in the mounds.

## AUTOMOBILE INDUSTRY
The manufacturing of transportation equipment is the largest industry in Ohio. The state produces more buses and trucks than any other state, as well as a high percentage of automobiles. Overall Ohio ranks third in the United States in manufacturing.

## FIRST MAN ON THE MOON
Neil Armstrong uttered the memorable phrase, "That's one small step for a man, one giant leap for mankind," as he became the first man to set foot on the moon on July 20, 1969. He was born in Ohio and began his carrier as a Navy pilot. Armstrong joined the space program as an astronaut in 1962. His initial mission, in 1966 in Gemini 8, involved the first docking in space. With Edwin Aldrin and Michael Collins he made the Apollo 11 moon mission.

# OKLAHOMA

The outline of Oklahoma looks like a clenched fist with a pointing finger. The finger, or panhandle (a strip of land that stretches out from the main region like the handle of a pan), extends for 175 miles (282km) to the New Mexico border. Most of the land is gently rolling prairie but has suffered badly from soil erosion, and in the 1930s terrible windstorms blew much of the topsoil away, creating the famous "Dust Bowl." A great deal of land has since been reclaimed. In the dry areas of the state, the main crops are wheat and hay; in the humid zones, sorghum, peanuts, and cotton are grown. Like Texas to the south, Oklahoma derives most of its farm income from cattle ranching, and it is also an oil state. Its manufacturing industries produce machinery, plastics, and rubber goods.

A state rich in Native American, cowboy, and homesteader history, Oklahoma's name comes from a Choctaw tribe word meaning "red people," and the land was originally the home of many Native American tribes, including the Comanche and Osage. The "Five Civilized Tribes"—Cherokee, Chickasaw, Choctaw, Creek, and Seminole—were forced by the government to settle there, and the territory was designated Native American land. But on April 22, 1889, the territory was opened up for settlement by homesteaders. Thousands of people on horseback and in covered wagons lined up to begin, literally, a race to stake land claims and to build homesteads. By nightfall some 10,000 settlers had poured onto the land. Some, however, had "jumped the gun" and staked land illegally. They were called "sooners," from which the state gets its nickname. Despite this land seizure, the state today holds the second-highest Native American population of any state— around 400,000.

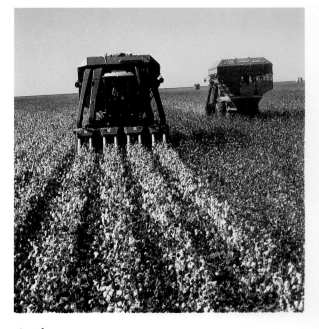

**COTTON PICKING**
Oklahoma's Red River region in the southeast corner of the state forms part of the fertile lowlands that stretch south, eventually reaching the Gulf of Mexico, and which provide fertile ground for growing cotton. Grains, dairy products, and livestock outrank cotton in terms of income, but this staple crop is important to the state's economy. The southeast corner, where the cotton is grown, has a humid climate and has been called "Little Dixie."

*STATE SYMBOLS*

*Redbud*

*Mistletoe*

*Scissor-tailored flycatcher*

**COWBOY COMEDIAN**
Actor and cowboy comedian Will Rogers was a famous Oklahoman entertainer of the early 1900s. Born in 1879, he developed a stage act, combining rope tricks with humorous comments about events of the time. In 1926 President Coolidge sent Rogers overseas as an "ambassador of good will."

**TOWERING TULSA**
In the 1920s Tulsa had more millionaires than any other city in the United States. Their wealth came chiefly from oil and from other minerals extracted around the city. This metallic-looking building is the City of Faith Medical Center, which rises 60 stories. Beside it are the research center and hospital. Tulsa is also an arts center, with its own ballet company, opera, and symphony orchestra. It has some fine museums, including an Institute of American History and Art.

COLORADO
NEW MEXICO
Δ Black Mesa
4,973 ft (1,517 m)
Boise City
Gunyon
KANSAS
North Canadian R.
Cimarron R.
Alva
Woodward
Blackwell
Ponca City
Enic
35
Arkansas R.
Bartlesville
Tulsa
Vinita
Miami
MISSOURI
Lake o' the Cherokees
SEQUOYAH STATE PARK
44
Clinton
Guthrie
Oklahoma City *
Muskogee
Elk City
40
Canadian R.
Norman
Shawnee
40
Chickasha
Anadarko
Eufaula Lake
McAlester
44
Altus
Lawton
Duncan
CHICKASAW NAT. RECREATION AREA
35
Lake Texoma
Valliant
Ardmore
Durant
Red R.
Idabel
ARKANSAS
TEXAS

0 100 kilometers
0 50 miles

## OKLAHOMA OIL

An oil refinery in Oklahoma. The discovery and exploitation of oil made Oklahoma rich, before petroleum was drilled in neighboring Texas. The first oil well began production on April 15, 1897, near Bartlesville, and the state produces over 6.6 million barrels of oil a year. Oil wells pump daily even inside Oklahoma City's limits, and wells surround the state Capitol Building. One well had to be drilled at an angle so that oil could be extracted from directly under the building. Oklahoma City was once dubbed "Oil Capital of the World." Oil is also drilled around Tulsa.

## CATTLE LANDS

Oklahoma supports some 87,000 farms. Cattle are the state's most valuable agricultural product, and livestock ranks first in terms of farming income. Irrigation schemes have helped farmers keep both their crops and their livestock supplied with water. Although Oklahoma is a serious rival to Texas in oil production, the number of cattle it raises is still less than half the number raised by Texas.

## OKLAHOMA

**Capital**
Oklahoma City
**Area**
69,898 sq. mi.
(181,022 sq. km)
**Population**
3,617,316 (2007)
**Largest cities**
Oklahoma City (547,274)
Tulsa (384,037)
**Statehood**
November 16, 1907
Rank: 46th
**Principal rivers**
Red, Arkansas,
Cimarron, Canadian
**Highest point**
Black Mesa
4,973 feet (1,517m)
**Motto**
*Labor Omnia Vincit*
(Work Conquers
All Things)
**Song**
"Oklahoma!"

## "TRAIL OF TEARS"

The Cherokees were one of the "Five Civilized Tribes" that settled in Oklahoma in the 1830s. This illustration shows the tribes being forced by the U.S. government to move from their original homelands in North Carolina and northern Georgia to what was intended to be a permanent Native American territory, occupying part of present-day Oklahoma. Some 15,000 Cherokees took the "Trail of Tears," where over 4,000 died from cold and disease. They were told that the new land was theirs, "as long as the grass grows and the waters run." But settlers moved into the territory, outnumbering Native Americans by five to one in 1905. Oklahoma was admitted to the Union as a state in 1907.

# OREGON

A Pacific Northwest state, Oregon is a land of stunning scenery and vast tracts of timber. It lies north of California, and like California has a long coastline. Unlike Californians, most of whom live along the coast, Oregon's inhabitants live mainly in the fertile inland area of their state, in the Willamette Valley. Also unlike California, most of Oregon's shoreline is public property, open to all. Oregon is the chief timber-producing state of the Union and is mainly rural. Industry is centered around lumber, used for wood and paper products. The redwood tree is perhaps the most valuable hardwood for the construction industry. Most of the state's forests are found in the Cascade and Coast mountain ranges. They are mainly evergreens, including Douglas fir—one of the state's symbols.

Other industries include food processing and manufacturing of scientific instruments. The state also produces a large amount of hydroelectric power. Fruit and vegetables are grown in the Willamette Valley. Winemaking is also well established, and the wines of Washington and Yamhill counties in the northwest are rated among the finest in the country. Wheat is the main crop in the eastern half of the state. The Cascade Range, named for its many waterfalls, divides the milder, misty, and wet coastal area from the dry, harsher climate of eastern Oregon. In the west the primary industry is fishing, especially of wild and farmed trout and salmon. Pacific Ocean fishing is as important now as it was to the Chinook tribe that first inhabited the region. Dairy cattle are raised in the Tillamook Valley.

Oregon's spectacular scenery includes the Painted Hills National Monument, the John Day Fossil Beds National Monument, and the spectacular Columbia River Gorge. The mouth of the river was first explored by Lewis and Clark in 1805. Settlers followed in the 1840s via the famous Oregon Trail, and the land became a U.S. territory in 1849.

## CRATER LAKE
Crater Lake is aptly named, as it was formed in a collapsed crater at the summit of an extinct volcano called Mt. Mazama. The lake is a brilliant deep-blue color due to the great depth of the water. It is the centerpiece of the state's only national park. At 1,962 feet (598m), Crater Lake is the deepest lake in the United States. There is a two-lane highway which goes around a nearby rim offering spectacular views of the lake 2,000 feet (610m) below.

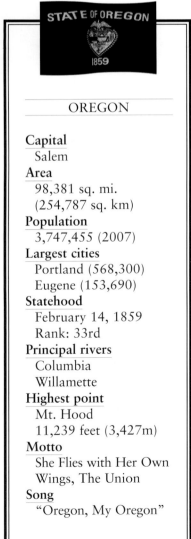

### OREGON

**Capital**
Salem
**Area**
98,381 sq. mi.
(254,787 sq. km)
**Population**
3,747,455 (2007)
**Largest cities**
Portland (568,300)
Eugene (153,690)
**Statehood**
February 14, 1859
Rank: 33rd
**Principal rivers**
Columbia
Willamette
**Highest point**
Mt. Hood
11,239 feet (3,427m)
**Motto**
She Flies with Her Own Wings, The Union
**Song**
"Oregon, My Oregon"

*Oregon grape*

*STATE SYMBOLS*

*Western meadowlark*

*Douglas fir*

## PORTLAND
The largest city in the state is Portland, which straddles the Willamette River. It is often called the "City of Roses" because it has an abundance of parks with beds of roses—and also rhododendrons. On a clear day, by the riverfront you can see the state's highest point, Mt. Hood, as well as the volcano Mt. St. Helens in Washington state, which erupted with terrifying force on May 18, 1980, and more recently had minor eruptions in late 2004. The explosion in 1980 was 500 times as powerful as the atomic bomb dropped on Hiroshima. Portland offers several museums and a large zoo.

## THE OREGON TRAIL

The historic Oregon Trail was an important route for settlers making their way west on horseback or by covered wagon in the 1840s–1870s. It stretches 2,000 miles (3,200km) from Independence, Missouri, across the Great Plains and Rocky Mountains into the present-day Oregon. Fur trappers and traders established part of the trail around the beginning of the 1800s. They were followed by missionaries and many other settlers, who were lured by the farming opportunities of the Willamette Valley. The end of the trail is marked by a stone in The Dalles on the northern Oregon border.

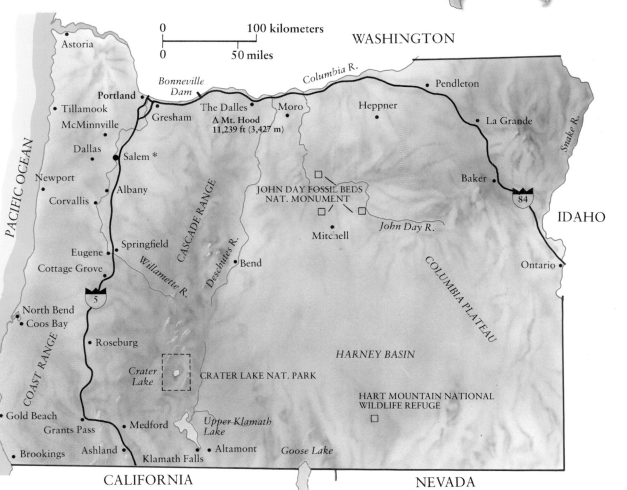

## MT. HOOD

At 11,239 feet (3,427m) Mt. Hood is the highest mountain in Oregon. Here its snow-covered peak towers in the distance beyond a typical apple orchard in full bloom. Mt. Hood is part of the Cascade Range, which has high slopes covered with evergreen forests. The mountain lies 45 miles (72km) from Portland and is a dormant volcano which last erupted in 1865. It was first sighted by an English navigator, William Broughton, who named it after the British admiral Lord Hood.

## GOLDEN EAGLE

The Pacific coast and interior wilderness of Oregon are ideal habitats for the golden eagle. It prefers the open, mountainous country that is typical of this state. This eagle is not really gold in color, but it has a few flecks of gold on its neck.

## STATE OF FLOWERS

Vivid yellow and red tulips grown in this nursery farm below the snow-capped Mt. Hood in the distance. Flower growing is an important part of the Oregon economy, especially in the Willamette Valley region. Other crops grown by farmers include cranberries, filberts, walnuts, and pears. Visitors drive along the many highways to see Oregon's flowers, parks, and spectacular mountain and coastal scenery.

# PENNSYLVANIA

The Northeastern state of Pennsylvania is crisscrossed by both the Appalachian and Allegheny mountains and borders Lake Erie. It is one of the top five industrial states in the Union, particularly in mining, and also has the sixth-highest population in the country. Because of its central location, with six states to the north and six to the south, Pennsylvania has the nickname "Keystone State."

In manufacturing Pennsylvania remains best known for its steel output. Pittsburgh, in the western part of the state, is the leading steel city in the United States, despite feeling the effects of an economic slump in the late 1970s and early 1980s. The state had its first steel mill, established by the industrialist Andrew Carnegie, in 1853. It also had the first developed oil field, and in the following decades Pennsylvania became a major industrial area, manufacturing iron, steel, arms, and machinery. Pennsylvania's mineral products include Portland cement, stone, pig iron, and lime. It is also one of the country's leading glassmaking states. The state produces automobiles and is the leading producer in the country of frozen dairy products, including ice cream. Other food products made in Pennsylvania include beer and chocolate. In recent years the state has also developed nuclear power. On March 28, 1979, the first serious nuclear accident in the United States occurred on Three Mile Island on the Susquehanna River, requiring a total shutdown of the power plant.

Dutch and Swedish settlers were the first Europeans in the region, but in 1682 an English colony was founded by William Penn for the Quakers, a Protestant sect seeking religious freedom. He founded Philadelphia, the largest city in Pennsylvania and sixth-largest in the nation. Penn's name for the city means "city of brotherly love" in Greek. Philadelphia's Independence Hall was the meeting place of the Continental Congress, which issued the Declaration of Independence—signed on July 4, 1776—and directed the war effort. Here, too, the U.S. Constitution was drawn up in 1787. From 1790 to 1800 the city served as the nation's first capital.

### GETTYSBURG ADDRESS

On November 19, 1863, President Abraham Lincoln delivered his most famous speech, the Gettysburg Address. The speech, which lasted only about two minutes, was given to dedicate a cemetery in Gettysburg for the soldiers who had died in the battle there in July of that year. Lincoln eloquently expressed the reasons for fighting the Civil War, ending with the words "... that government of the people, by the people, for the people, shall not perish from the earth."

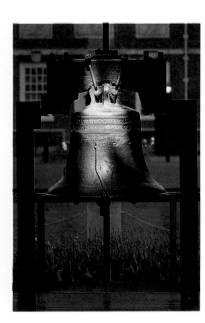

### LIBERTY BELL

Although it now has a new home, the Liberty Bell stood for many years in Liberty Bell Pavilion, which was built for Philadelphia's Bicentennial celebrations in 1976. The bell itself was cast in London to commemorate 50 years of Pennsylvania as a colony. It reached Philadelphia in 1752, and one month later was cracked by a stroke of its clapper. It was recast by a local firm and used to announce that the Continental Congress was in session and to proclaim the first public reading of the Declaration of Independence. It cracked again in 1835, but was not recast.

*STATE SYMBOLS*

*Hemlock*

*Mountain laurel*

*Ruffed grouse*

## PENNSYLVANIA

**Capital**
Harrisburg
**Area**
46,055 sq. mi.
(119,273 sq. km)
**Population**
12,432,792 (2007)
**Largest cities**
Philadelphia (1,449,634)
Pittsburgh (312,819)
**Statehood**
December 12, 1787
Rank: 2nd
**Principal rivers**
Allegheny, Ohio,
Susquehanna, Delaware
**Highest point**
Mt. Davis
3,213 feet (980m)
**Motto**
Virtue, Liberty,
and Independence
**Song**
None

## PITTSBURGH

Skyscrapers, such as this impressive example, dominate the Pittsburgh skyline. One Pittsburgh skyscraper, the U.S. Steel Building, is the tallest between New York City and Chicago. There is a mass of skyscrapers in the Golden Triangle, where the Allegheny, Monongahela, and Ohio rivers meet.

## AMISH WAYS

An Amish couple transports their harvest in the traditional, non-mechanized way of their sect. The Amish do not use automobiles, tractors, electricity, or any modern machinery. They live and work simply, gathering to worship at each other's houses twice a week. Amish people are not allowed to hold public office, swear oaths, or join the army. They are descendants of German immigrants from the Rhine region, who settled in large numbers in the inland counties, such as Lancaster. By the time of the Revolutionary War, these Germans were known as Pennsylvania Dutch. The word "Dutch" was taken from *deutsch*, meaning German (not people from The Netherlands). The Amish are just one—albeit the best known—of the German religious sects that settled in Pennsylvania.

## MARY CASSATT

The painter Mary Cassatt was born in Pittsburgh, Pennsylvania, in 1844 but moved to France when she was 22 years old. There she studied with the famous Impressionist painters, including Edgar Degas. She worked chiefly in pastels and made many fine figure studies of young women and mothers. This is her tender study of *Mother and Child*. Many of her works were of motherhood. She persuaded some of her wealthy American friends to buy Impressionist paintings and so helped influence American art appreciation.

## PUMPKIN PRODUCER

Pennsylvania is one of the leading pumpkin producers east of the Mississippi River. Freshly harvested pumpkins are shipped out for use either as cattle feed or for human consumption—particularly the pulp, which is boiled or baked in pies, traditionally served at Thanksgiving. Pumpkins are closely related to cucumbers, squashes, and melons.

# RHODE ISLAND

The smallest state in the nation, Rhode Island measures a mere 48 miles (77km) from north to south and 37 miles (60km) from east to west. But its population density—the number of people for each square mile—is the second highest in the United States. Some 75 percent of the population live within 15 miles (24km) of the capital and largest city, Providence. This city is the third largest in New England and is located in the eastern part of the state, at the head of Narragansett Bay. Around one third of the population works in the manufacturing industries, making Rhode Island one of the most industrialized states in the nation. Textiles, metal-working machinery, chemicals, plastics, electrical equipment, silverware, and costume jewelry are the main products. The state leads the world in the manufacture of the latter two items. Textiles once accounted for half of the state income, but competition from southern mills and from overseas reduced this. One of Rhode Island's symbols is the Rhode Island Red chicken, bred t here from 1857 and a producer of excellent eggs. Small dairy farms and nurseries are other significant agricultural activities, and potatoes, corn, apples, and peaches are also grown.

The colony of Rhode Island was founded by Roger Williams, who had been expelled from the Massachusetts Bay Colony in 1636. Several denominations built their first houses of worship there. The Touro Synagogue, which was built in 1763 in Newport, is the oldest synagogue in the United States. In 1776 Rhode Island was the first colony to formally declare its independence from England but the last of the original Thirteen Colonies to join the new Union.

GRAND MANSIONS
America's richest families built grand French- and Italian-style mansions (their summer houses) along a 3-mile (5-km) cliff stretch of Newport, Rhode Island. The families—the Astors, Vanderbilts, and Belmonts —had made their wealth from the large-scale industrialization of the nation in 1800s. Typical of these "cottages" (as their owners called them) is The Breakers (above) designed for the industrialist Cornelius Vanderbilt and his family.

STATE SYMBOLS

Violet

Red maple

Rhode Island Red

NEWPORT
Newport was founded in 1639 and became the first American resort, with wealthy merchants vacationing here as early as the 1720s. The resort, reached by the impressive Newport Bridge, boasts the International Lawn Tennis Hall of Fame, a casino, and the White Horse Tavern, claimed as the country's oldest.

FOUNDERS OF RHODE ISLAND
In 1636 Roger Williams established Rhode Island's first permanent settlement in Providence. Williams was a Puritan minister who was driven out of Massachusetts because he attacked the Puritan leaders for not practicing religious tolerance. Providence was built on land Williams bought from two Narragansett chiefs. Setting up a new colony was fraught with dangers—land had to be cleared even in the harsh New England winter, and supplies were scarce. By 1643 there were four settlements in Rhode Island and Williams suggested that they unite for protection against neighboring colonies. In 1663 King Charles II of England granted Rhode Island a charter under which the settlements united. This charter remained the law of Rhode Island until 1843.

## RHODE ISLAND

**Capital**
Providence
**Area**
1,045 sq. mi.
(2,706 sq. km)
**Population**
1,057,832 (2007)
**Largest cities**
Providence (175,255)
Warwick (87,233)
**Statehood**
May 29, 1790
Rank: 13th
**Principal rivers**
Providence, Blackstone
**Highest point**
Jerimoth Hill
812 feet (248m)
**Motto**
Hope
**Song**
"Rhode Island"

### CENTER FOR SAILING
Newport is a yachting center, and many yacht races are held there, including some of the world-famous America's Cup races. In late June there is the annual Block Island Race and the Newport to Bermuda and Annapolis to Newport races. Sport fishing is also popular in the Ocean State. The waters off Rhode Island provide large fish such as tuna and smaller fish such as mackerel and bluefish.

### COASTAL BIRDS
Gulls and terns are common along Rhode Island's shoreline. The herring gull is the best-known gull in the United States. The Caspian tern is smaller and faster.

*Caspain tern*

*Herring gull*

### PAWTUCKET
Copper wiring is processed in Pawtucket, close to Providence, the capital of Rhode Island. Pawtucket is a major producer of textiles, machinery, and plastics, as well as copper wire. It is also a center for high-tech industries and toy manufacturing.

### BROWN UNIVERSITY
Rhode Island's oldest institution of higher education is Brown University in Providence. It was founded in 1764 as a college for Baptist men. It began to admit women in 1971. Brown is a private institution and one of the Ivy League colleges. Computer and information sciences, engineering, languages, mathematics, and psychology are among the subjects taught there. The first schools in Rhode Island were set up and supported financially by the main towns. State-supported colleges include the University of Rhode Island in Kingston and the Rhode Island School of Design. The latter is world famous.

# SOUTH CAROLINA

One of the original 13 states of the Union, South Carolina is located in the southeastern United States. It is shaped roughly like a triangle and has a 187-mile (301-km) Atlantic coastline. Georgia lies on its southwest border, while North Carolina runs along its north and northeast border. South Carolina has played a key role in American history: it led the Southern states in breaking away from the Union and into the Civil War. The shots fired at Fort Sumter in Charleston Harbor in 1861 sparked the war. The state's wealth came from its slave-based rice, indigo, and cotton trade, and the wealth of the planters was equal to that of the northern industrialists. Charleston itself was badly damaged in the Civil War, but many of the wealthy merchants' mansions have been restored. The gardens of the old Charleston homes are at their best in spring, when the magnolias and other flowers come into bloom. Charleston Museum, established in 1773, is the oldest in the United States. There is also an Old Slave Museum, which is the oldest museum devoted to African-American culture. It vividly evokes the horrors of slave trading, depicting shackled slaves coming off their crammed ships. Nearby is Charles Towne Landing—named after the English King Charles II—where the first British colonists settled in 1670. These settlers were mainly poor whites from Barbados, who managed only a precarious existence. Later, exiled Huguenots (French Protestants) arrived and started rice plantations, worked by slave labor. The invention of the cotton gin in 1793 established cotton as the leading crop until the Civil War.

The coastal plain covers two-thirds of the state. In the northwest corner are the Blue Ridge Mountains. The rest of the state is part of the Piedmont Plateau. South Carolina has a hot, humid climate favoring the cultivation of tobacco and soybeans, as well as corn, cotton, and peaches.

CHARLESTON
Many restored old houses along Charleston's harbor were built in the 1700s for sea captains and merchants. Charleston is a busy port and the largest city in the eastern lowland area. It was the first permanent settlement in what is now South Carolina. It started as Charles Towne in 1670 and was moved to its present location between the Ashley and Cooper rivers ten years later.

## SOUTH CAROLINA

**Capital**
Columbia
**Area**
32,020 sq. mi.
(82,925 sq. km)
**Population**
4,407,709 (2007)
**Largest cities**
Columbia (124,818)
Charleston (118,492)
**Statehood**
May 23, 1788
Rank: 8th
**Principal rivers**
Santee, Edisto,
Savannah
**Highest point**
Sassafras Mountain
3,560 feet (1,086m)
**Motto**
*Dum Spiro Spero*
(While I Breathe, I Hope)
**Song**
"Carolina"

TABLE ROCK
A mountain lake in northwest South Carolina reflects Table Rock, part of the Blue Ridge chain of the Appalachian Mountains. The Blue Ridge region is a small area tucked away in the far northwest corner. It offers spectacular scenery but does not contribute to the state's economy. The Blue Ridge Mountains enter from North Carolina and contain Sassafras Mountain, at 3,560 feet (1,086m) the state's highest peak.

*STATE SYMBOLS*

*Carolina wren*

*Palmetto*

*Carolina jessamine*

## THE TEXTILE STATE
A typical garment factory in South Carolina. Textiles and clothing are important manufactured goods in this cotton-growing state. However, the textile industry depends less on cotton today than on synthetic fibers, such as nylon and rayon. The state has supported schools to train workers for this industry—there were over 400 such establishments in the 1980s, employing about 30 percent of the textile work force. Textile mills are concentrated in the northwest of the state. The industry began in the 1820s, when cotton was firmly established as the state's foremost crop, grown on large plantations.

## KIAWAH ISLAND
This large island, part of a coastal chain of barrier islands, is not far from Charleston and includes wildlife refuge areas, forests, marshlands, and isolated beaches, as well as a historic private mansion. In 1991 the island was also the site of the Ryder Cup, a golf tournament held every two years, in which a team of the best of America's golfers takes on the best golfing team from all parts of Europe. Apart from trying to win the trophy for their team, the golfers also had to keep an eye out for the many alligators that lurk around the golf course greens and fairways.

## PEACHES
One of the state's main crops is peaches. They were introduced by Spanish explorers. Cultivated fruit trees thrive in the state's warm climate.

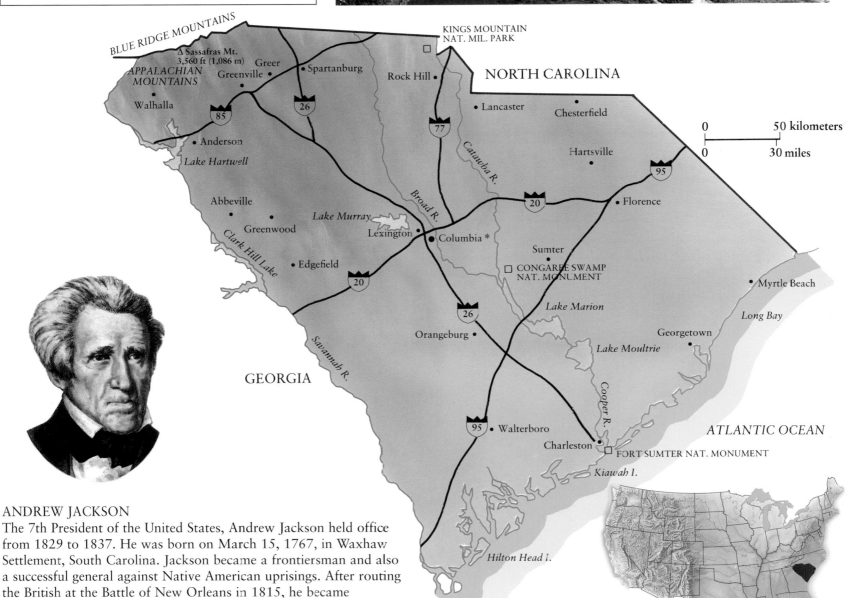

## ANDREW JACKSON
The 7th President of the United States, Andrew Jackson held office from 1829 to 1837. He was born on March 15, 1767, in Waxhaw Settlement, South Carolina. Jackson became a frontiersman and also a successful general against Native American uprisings. After routing the British at the Battle of New Orleans in 1815, he became a national hero. He was a supporter of states' rights.

# SOUTH DAKOTA

Geographically, South Dakota is almost like two states divided down the center by the Missouri River. East of the Missouri is rich, rolling farmland, where farmers grow corn, wheat, soybeans, and alfalfa. But there are also glacial lakes to the north. West of the Missouri is seemingly endless prairie with few trees. It is here, to the southwest, that South Dakota's most elevated region, the Black Hills, lies. These hills extend for some 120 miles (193km) from north to south and 60 miles (97km) from east to west; their granite peaks rise 4,000 feet (1,200m) above the surrounding plains. Mt. Rushmore is located here. Next to the Black Hills are the barren but stunning Badlands, a region of jagged cliffs and ravines. The largest area of Badlands in South Dakota lies between the Cheyenne and White rivers. As in neighboring North Dakota the weather is harsh, with hot summers and cold winters. There is a feeling of open space throughout this sparsely populated state, and over 90 percent of the land is suitable for farming. However, the state suffers from periodic drought, frosts, and blizzards. It also felt the full force of the "Dust Bowl" of the 1930s, when severe winds whipped off the fertile topsoil and brought great suffering to the people of the state. Today South Dakota's agriculture is thriving. Livestock raising, especially of beef cattle, is important to western South Dakota. The territory of South Dakota was obtained from the French in 1803 as part of the Louisiana Purchase. It was traditionally Sioux territory, and until the 1870s, when gold was discovered, it attracted relatively few settlers—mainly fur traders and farmers.

CUSTER STATE PARK
A bison mother suckles her calf unperturbed in Custer State Park, an area of mountains, forests, and lakes. Other animals found in the park include antelope, deer, and elk, all of which roam the range.

*Ringed-necked pheasant*

STATE SYMBOLS

*American pasqueflower*

*Black Hills spruce*

CALAMITY JANE
Martha Jane Burke was a frontierswoman who, under the nickname of Calamity Jane, became a famous Wild West character. In 1876 she moved to Deadwood, South Dakota, and became a bullwhacker, hauling goods to the gold mining camps.

GIANT SCULPTURES
The heads of four presidents are carved in the side of Mt. Rushmore in the Black Hills of South Dakota. The "Shrine of Democracy," as it is known, is part of Mt. Rushmore National Memorial. The faces are 70 feet (21m) high. Visitors approach the sculpted heads along a scenic route called the Iron Mountain Road, which zigzags up steep slopes with several bridges and tunnels.

## SOUTH DAKOTA

**Capital**
Pierre
**Area**
77,116 sq. mi.
(199,715 sq. km)
**Population**
796,214 (2007)
**Largest cities**
Sioux Falls (151,505)
Rapid City (63,997)
**Statehood**
November 2, 1889
Rank: 40th
**Principal rivers**
Cheyenne, White,
Missouri
**Highest point**
Harney Peak
7,242 feet (2,209m)
**Motto**
Under God,
the People Rule
**Song**
"Hail, South Dakota"

NORTH DAKOTA

MONTANA

Ladner
• Buffalo
• Camp Crook

*Grand R.*

Eureka

• Mobridge

**Aberdeen** •

• Britton
Sisseton

*Big Stone Lake*

GREAT PLAINS

*Lake Oahe*

Watertown

• Clark

MINNESOTA

Belle Fourche

*Cheyenne R.*

• Okobojo

• Pierre *

Huron

Brookings

Howard

Deadwood
• Sturgis
Lead
Rapid City

MT. RUSHMORE NAT. MEMORIAL

Madison

29

△
Harney Peak
7,242 ft (2,209 m)

CUSTER STATE
PARK

BADLANDS
NAT. PARK

I-90

Dell Rapids
Salem

WYOMING

WIND CAVE
NAT. PARK

*White R.*

Mitchell

Sioux Falls

BLACK
HILLS

Hot Springs

*Lake Francis Case*

JEWEL CAVE
NAT. MONUMENT

Wounded Knee

• Pine Ridge

• Martin

*Missouri R.*

Fairfax

Tyndell

Yankton

*Big Sioux R.*

0        100 kilometers
0        50 miles

NEBRASKA

Vermillion

IOWA

## DAKOTA

*Dakota,* or "allies," was the name the Sioux gave themselves and tribes friendly to them. Today the Sioux make up over seven percent of South Dakota's population. This man is dressed in the traditional costume of the Sioux.

## MAMMOTH REMAINS

Visitors inspect the remains of extinct Ice Age mammoths at Mammoth Site, Hot Springs, in the southwest corner of South Dakota. Mammoth bones that have been preserved for 10,000 years are on display at this site. The mammoth was a prehistoric relative of the elephant. It existed until relatively recently, dying out a mere 10,000 years ago. Earlier animals that roamed the North American continent include brontotheres, which looked similar to a rhinoceros, saber-toothed cats, and ancestors of pronghorn antelopes, pigs, sheep, and cattle. Hot Springs itself is suitably named for its large, still-bubbling springs. The Sioux fought the Cheyenne over the land rights for these springs.

## PRAIRIE DOGS

As its name suggests the prairie dog is found on the prairies, particularly on the plains of South Dakota. It is a type of squirrel that lives in the ground in large groups known as colonies, or "towns." In their underground colonies, linked by a network of tunnels, the animals groom each other and appear to kiss. If an enemy such as a rattlesnake or coyote comes close, the prairie dogs will warn others in the colony with loud, sharp, barking calls. The openings to the burrows are surrounded by mounds of earth to prevent the burrows from flooding.

## GOLD MINING

A miner at work in a South Dakota gold mine. The Homestake Mine, just north of Rapid City in western South Dakota, is the most profitable gold mine in the United States. Surface tours are available for sightseers. Mining in general, however, makes up only a very small percentage of the state's income. There are many old "gold rush" towns where the mines are no longer working. Some of these are open to visitors.

# TENNESSEE

A land of music and mountains, Tennessee is a long, narrow Southern state lying in the east-central part of the United States. It extends from the Great Smoky Mountains in eastern Tennessee over 432 miles (695km) to the Mississippi River. Tennessee is bordered by eight states: to the north are Kentucky and Virginia; to the south Georgia, Alabama, and Mississippi; to the west lie Missouri and Arkansas; and to the east is North Carolina. The Great Smoky Mountains have magnificent plants and wildlife and are crisscrossed with whitewater creeks and rivers. The construction of a number of dams on the Tennessee River was a project of the Tennessee Valley Authority (TVA), an agency set up and financed by the federal government as part of the New Deal during the Depression of the 1930s. The project tamed the Tennessee River and provided plentiful power for industry, and the dams formed a number of lakes, including Cherokee Lake.

Once a mainly rural state known chiefly for its dairy products, Tennessee has become increasingly industrialized. Chemicals and machinery are the primary products, and there is also a large cottonseed-oil business based in Memphis, the largest city. In the past, Tennessee's main crop was cotton, but it has been surpassed by soybeans and tobacco. There is cattle raising in the state, as well as breeding of the Tennessee Walking horse, a famous breed of saddle horse. There is also an automobile industry and an important center for nuclear research at Oak Ridge. Tourism is a thriving industry in the state. Vacationers come to see the beautiful countryside and enjoy the state's musical heritage. Tennessee is both the birthplace of the blues and the capital of country and western music. During the Civil War the state was the site of many battles.

**STATE SYMBOLS**

*Mockingbird*

*Iris*

*Tulip poplar*

| TENNESSEE |
|---|
| **Capital** |
| Nashville |
| **Area** |
| 42,143 sq. mi. |
| (109,142 sq. km) |
| **Population** |
| 6,156,719 (2007) |
| **Largest cities** |
| Memphis (647,028) |
| Nashville-Davidson |
| (619,626) |
| **Statehood** |
| June 1, 1796 |
| Rank: 16th |
| **Principal rivers** |
| Tennessee, Mississippi |
| **Highest point** |
| Clingmans Dome |
| 6,643 feet (2,026m) |
| **Motto** |
| Agriculture and |
| Commerce |
| **Song** |
| "The Tennessee Waltz" |

NASHVILLE SKYLINE
Tennessee's capital occupies hilly ground along the Cumberland River near the center of the state. It is best known as the home of American country and western music. The Grand Ole Opry House, a large concert hall, has presented many of the most famous country and western artists including Roy Rogers, Johnny Cash, and Dolly Patron.

ELVIS PRESLEY
Elvis Aaron Presley was born in Tupelo, Mississippi, but after achieving fame he settled on a vast estate named Graceland in Memphis. He died in the mansion on August 16, 1977. Eight million of his records were sold in the week after his death. Elvis was the supreme performer of the Rock'n'Roll music of the mid-1950s. The studios of Sun Records, where Elvis and other artists launched the songs that were to transform the sound and look of popular music, are in Memphis.

## ATHENS OF THE SOUTH
Nashville is sometimes referred to as the "Athens of the South" because of its many colleges and universities and for its Greek Revival architecture—buildings that copy the style of the Ancient Greek cities. Located in Centennial Park, this building is the world's only full-scale replica of the Parthenon temple in Athens, Greece.

## AUTOMOBILES
Several new, large, high-tech motor vehicle plants have been built near Nashville, including some making Japanese automobiles, such as these Nissan trucks. Trucks and cars from Japan have cut greatly into the sales and production of American cars. Other Nashville industries include food processing, glassmaking, and recordings. More than 180 record companies are located here.

## WILD TURKEYS
The wild turkey is a native bird of North America. It lives in woodlands in parts of the central, southern, and eastern United States, including Tennessee as well as North Carolina and Minnesota. It is a different species from the domestic turkey, traditionally served for Thanksgiving and Christmas dinners.

## CUMBERLAND GAP
Pinnacle Overlook in the Cumberland Gap National Historical Park offers spectacular views. At this point the borders of three state—Kentucky, Virginia, and Tennessee—meet. Cold, moist air or mist trapped by the Great Smoky Mountains often sweeps over the peaks. The mountains are part of the great Appalachian chain that extends from Canada in the north to Alabama in the south. Many pioneers passed through the Gap when moving west in the early 1700s and 1800s.

# TEXAS

Texas was the largest state in the Union until 1959, when Alaska became a state. It was also credited with the largest underground oil lake in the United States until larger reserves were discovered in Alaska. Texas remains the largest of the 48 contiguous states, and oil has made Texas among the richest states in the nation. It was in Spindletop, Texas, that the state's first great oil "gusher" erupted from the ground on January 10, 1901. It uncovered one of the most productive oil fields in the world. Today Texas leads all other states in the production of its most important natural resources—petroleum and cotton. The state also leads the world in oil-disaster rescue and cleanup operations, from tanker spillages to the burning oil wells of Kuwait sabotaged by Iraqi forces in the Persian Gulf War of 1991. Dallas is another oil city and is the banking center of the Southwest. The Dallas-Fort Worth area is a center for manufacturing, aerospace, and the electronics industry. Texas, however, is more than just oil wells and Stetson-hatted oilmen; it is also one of the most productive farming states in the Union. Cattle and cotton dominated the state before oil was discovered. In the past much of the farm work was done by African slaves and Mexicans—whose descendants, along with newcomers, form a sizable portion of today's population. Texas is a leading center for the nation's space flight programs. NASA's Lyndon B. Johnson Space Center in Houston was the "mission control" for the Mercury, Gemini, and Apollo space flights.

As a republic Texas acquired the flag it still flies today— a red, white, and blue flag bearing a single star—the inspiration for its nickname, "Lone Star State."

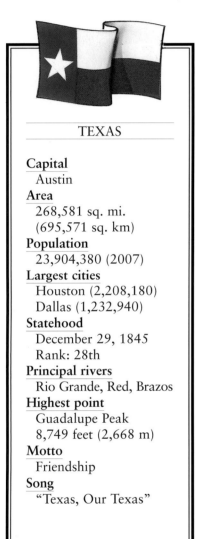

### TEXAS

**Capital**
Austin
**Area**
268,581 sq. mi.
(695,571 sq. km)
**Population**
23,904,380 (2007)
**Largest cities**
Houston (2,208,180)
Dallas (1,232,940)
**Statehood**
December 29, 1845
Rank: 28th
**Principal rivers**
Rio Grande, Red, Brazos
**Highest point**
Guadalupe Peak
8,749 feet (2,668 m)
**Motto**
Friendship
**Song**
"Texas, Our Texas"

## TEXAS BECOMES A STATE

The American flag was raised on Texas soil in 1845. Before this time, Texas had been a possession of Spain, then of Mexico, and then an independent republic. President James K. Polk was instrumental in acquiring Texas for the United States. The annexation of Texas and a dispute over the Texas–Mexico border triggered the Mexican War of 1846–1848.

## THE ALAMO

The Alamo was built by the Spanish as a mission in 1718. In 1835–1836 the people of Texas rebelled against the Mexican government who ruled over Texas. The Mexican army, led by General Santa Anna, marched on San Antonio. The Texans retreated to the Alamo, and a long siege followed. The Mexicans finally took the fort on March 6, 1836. Many died, including frontiersmen Davy Crockett, Jim Bowie, and William Travis.

## STATE SYMBOLS

*Mockingbird*

*Pecan*

*Bluebonnet*

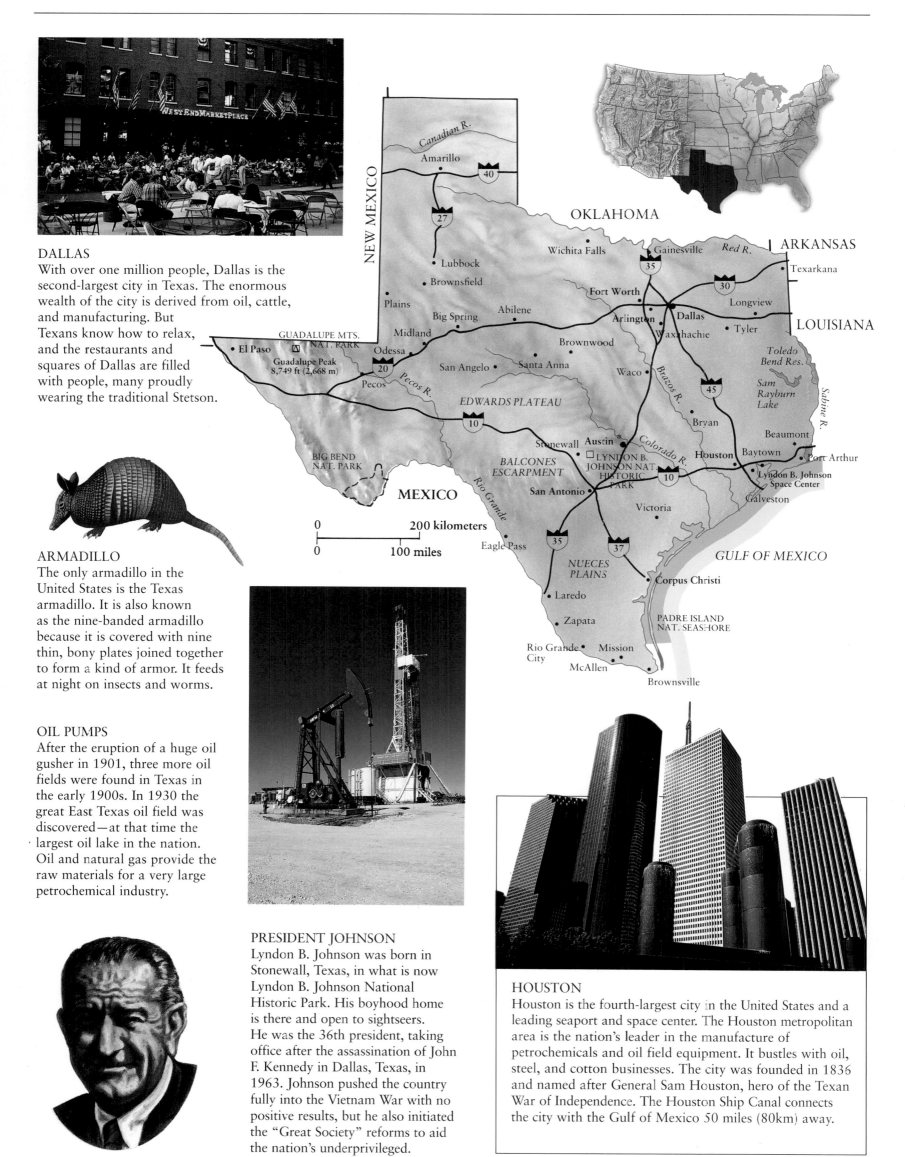

## DALLAS

With over one million people, Dallas is the second-largest city in Texas. The enormous wealth of the city is derived from oil, cattle, and manufacturing. But Texans know how to relax, and the restaurants and squares of Dallas are filled with people, many proudly wearing the traditional Stetson.

## ARMADILLO

The only armadillo in the United States is the Texas armadillo. It is also known as the nine-banded armadillo because it is covered with nine thin, bony plates joined together to form a kind of armor. It feeds at night on insects and worms.

## OIL PUMPS

After the eruption of a huge oil gusher in 1901, three more oil fields were found in Texas in the early 1900s. In 1930 the great East Texas oil field was discovered—at that time the largest oil lake in the nation. Oil and natural gas provide the raw materials for a very large petrochemical industry.

## PRESIDENT JOHNSON

Lyndon B. Johnson was born in Stonewall, Texas, in what is now Lyndon B. Johnson National Historic Park. His boyhood home is there and open to sightseers. He was the 36th president, taking office after the assassination of John F. Kennedy in Dallas, Texas, in 1963. Johnson pushed the country fully into the Vietnam War with no positive results, but he also initiated the "Great Society" reforms to aid the nation's underprivileged.

## HOUSTON

Houston is the fourth-largest city in the United States and a leading seaport and space center. The Houston metropolitan area is the nation's leader in the manufacture of petrochemicals and oil field equipment. It bustles with oil, steel, and cotton businesses. The city was founded in 1836 and named after General Sam Houston, hero of the Texan War of Independence. The Houston Ship Canal connects the city with the Gulf of Mexico 50 miles (80km) away.

# UTAH

Lying in the heart of the Rocky Mountains, Utah has a generally high elevation, with many high peaks; even its lowest point is 2,000 feet (610m) above sea level. At its southeast corner it meets three other states—New Mexico, Colorado, and Arizona. Utah is famous for its spectacular national parks, of which the best known are Bryce Canyon, Zion, and Arches. The strange rugged rock formations of these parks resulted from the action of the large glaciers that formed in prehistoric times and from erosion caused by flash foods pouring over the bare rocks. The Great Salt Lake in the northwest of the state is all that remains of what was once a vast inland sea.

Most of Utah is mountainous of semidesert. The arid Great Basin, which includes Great Salt Lake, occupies the western third. The rest of the state consists of the Rockies in the north and the Colorado Plateau in the south. The state produces a number of valuable minerals including oil, natural gas, coal, copper, iron ore, gold, and silver. Steelmaking, copper smelting, and oil refining are the main manufacturing activities. Utah's many farms and ranches have cattle and sheep, which are raised as livestock. Market dairy products are also important.

Fur trappers were among the first travelers in the region. The Mormons arrived in 1848, the year in which Utah became part of the United States as a result of the Mexican War. The region became a territory in 1850, with the Mormon leader Brigham Young as governor. It was named Utah after the Ute tribe who lived there along with Shoshone and Paiute tribes. The Mormons had called the region *Deseret*, a Mormon word meaning honeybee, which stands for hard work and industry. This is where Utah gets its nickname, the "Beehive State." In 1890 the church gave up the practice of polygamy, which allowed a man to have more than one wife, and this opened the way for Utah to become a state in 1896. Today the population is chiefly of European descent, the result of several Mormon migrations. Most people in the state live in a narrow belt stretching from Ogden to Provo.

*STATE SYMBOLS*

*Seagull*

*Sego lily*

*Blue spruce*

MORMON CITY
The six-spired Mormon Temple in Salt Lake City, capital of Utah and world center of the Mormon Church, took 40 years to build. Utah's story is linked to that of the Church of Jesus Christ of Latter-Day Saints.

BRYCE CANYON
Bryce Canyon National Park in the southern part of Utah was the state's first national park. Its pink cliffs, colored by iron and other minerals in the limestone, are spectacular and reveal layers of sediment deposits laid down over millions of years. The Paiute word for Bryce means "red rocks standing like men in a bowl-shaped canyon."

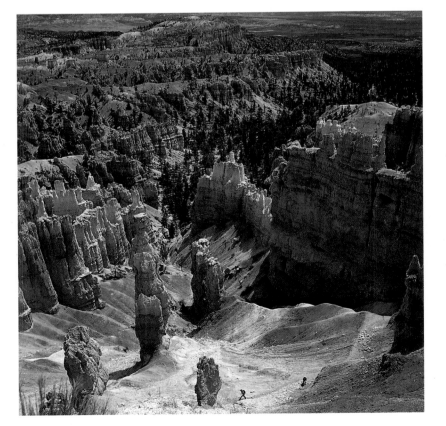

| UTAH | |
|---|---|
| **Capital** | |
| Salt Lake City | |
| **Area** | |
| 84,899 sq. mi. | |
| (219,871 sq. km) | |
| **Population** | |
| 2,645,330 (2007) | |
| **Largest cities** | |
| Salt Lake City (178,858) | |
| West Valley City | |
| (118,917) | |
| **Statehood** | |
| January 4, 1896 | |
| Rank: 45th | |
| **Principal rivers** | |
| Colorado | |
| Green | |
| **Highest point** | |
| Kings Peak | |
| 13,528 feet (4,126m) | |
| **Motto** | |
| Industry | |
| **Song** | |
| "Utah, We Love Thee" | |

IDAHO

WYOMING

NEVADA

COLORADO

ARIZONA

## COPPER MINE
Bingham Canyon is the site of the Kennecott open-pit copper mine—the largest in the world. This area of north-central Utah is rich in minerals, including coal, gold, silver, lead, uranium, and molybdenum. Copper is one of the most important minerals mined in Utah, and it is used in building and construction, electric and electronic manufacturing, and by industrial machinery and equipment makers. The U.S. is the world's second-largest producer.

## BOBCATS
Bobcats thrive in the mountain forests and stony terrain of the Rocky Mountain states, and Utah provides these habitats in abundance. Also called the lynx, the bobcat generally hunts at night, feeding on rodents, rabbits, birds, and sometimes deer.

## THE MORMON TRAIL
In July 1847 Brigham Young, the Mormon's leader, announced to his followers: "This is the right place"—having led them 1,300 miles (2,000 m) from Illinois. He was standing at what was to become Salt Lake City. To make this dry, salty land fertile, the Mormons created a network of irrigation channels to grow crops.

## NEWSPAPER ROCK
Early cave dwellers called the Anasazi have left amazing rock scratchings, called petroglyphs, at what is now the Newspaper Rock State Historical Monument. The carvings may have been a kind of news report for the inhabitants. Many of the petroglyphs are clearly etched and obvious to the untrained eye—including hands, feet, deer-hunting, mountain sheep, and sun signs. The Navajo word for this rock is *Tsi Haue*, "rock that tells a story." The site is located within Canyonlands National Park. To get there drivers pass through a narrow, verdant valley with towering sandstone walls.

# VERMONT

The name of this New England state, in the northeast corner of the country, comes from the French words *vert* and *mont*, which mean "green mountain"—the state's nickname. The Green Mountains of Vermont run north to south like a backbone along the center of the state. The width of the range varies from 20 to 36 miles (32 to 58km). The state's many mountain regions yield granite, marble, and other kinds of stones. However, such a rock-filled landscape also prevents farming from playing a major role in the state's economy. The state was first investigated by the French explorer Samuel de Champlain, whose name has been given to a lake and to the canal that links Vermont to the sea by connecting Lake Champlain to the Hudson River in New York state.

Vermont has a small, scattered population, and its countryside is well protected by environmental protection laws, passed as early as the 1970s, which also control all development within the state. There are 40 state parks and 34 state forests. Each year in the fall, visitors from out of state come to see the leaves turn spectacular shades of red and gold. Long winters and deep snow in the mountains attract many thousands of skiers to the 56 ski areas in the state. The two chief agricultural products are apples and maple syrup. The few thousand farms in the state are located mainly around Lake Champlain in the northwest or along the Connecticut River, which forms Vermont's eastern boundary. Milk from dairy cows is also a major product. Forests cover much of Vermont and provide the raw material for the state's thriving lumber industry. Quarrying began in the state in 1785, and large deposits of granite, marble, and slate are used in buildings throughout the nation.

*Sugar maple*

*Red clover*

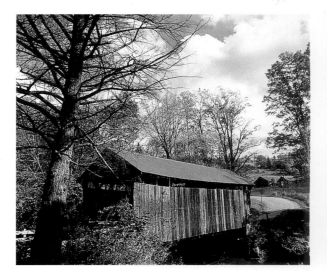

COVERED BRIDGE
This typical New England scene, a covered bridge surrounded by fall foliage, is set in peaceful farmland. There are over 100 of these historic bridges in Vermont alone. The largest concentration of them, totaling 16, can be found around Lamomile Country east of Burlington. Such bridges attract vacationers year-round and help make tourism a major source of the state's income. Visitors come to enjoy Vermont's invigorating climate, with hundreds of thousands of acres of protected forests, public recreation parks, and wildlife preserves.

STATE SYMBOLS

*Hermit thrush*

ETHAN ALLEN
In the 1750s Ethan Allen settled on land that is now in Vermont. This land was later given to New York by the British government. Allen formed the Green Mountain Boys to defend Vermont's land. During the Revolutionary War the Green Mountain Boys captured Fort Ticonderoga from the British.

GREEN MOUNTAINS
The Green Mountains form the spine of Vermont. Stunning fall foliage, high peaks, and 80–120 inches (200–305cm) of winter snow make them a key attraction of the state's tourist industry. From December to April thousands of people from all over the world flock to Vermont's ski resorts.

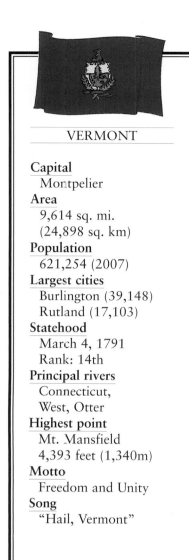

## VERMONT

**Capital**
Montpelier
**Area**
9,614 sq. mi.
(24,898 sq. km)
**Population**
621,254 (2007)
**Largest cities**
Burlington (39,148)
Rutland (17,103)
**Statehood**
March 4, 1791
Rank: 14th
**Principal rivers**
Connecticut,
West, Otter
**Highest point**
Mt. Mansfield
4,393 feet (1,340m)
**Motto**
Freedom and Unity
**Song**
"Hail, Vermont"

### NATURAL MAPLE

The sugar maple, one of America's most common trees, is the Vermont state tree. Maple trees have many uses apart from providing sugary sap; they give shade in summer and act as windbreaks for farmers. Maple is also a favorite wood for furniture makers because it is strong and polishes to a good shine. The winged maple seeds grow from branches in pairs like propellers they then separate and float to the ground.

### EXTRACTING MAPLE SYRUP

As winter turns to spring the sap in the sugar maples begins to rise, heralding "sugaring time." Millions of trees are tapped for the annual maple syrup harvest. The sap is sugared down in special buildings, where the water in the sap boils off in an evaporator. It takes the extract of four trees to produce 1 gallon (3.8 liters) of maple syrup. Because of this maple syrup is expensive. Several farms—most of which are primarily dairy farms—admit visitors to see the operation of their sugar houses.

### CALVIN COOLIDGE

John Calvin Coolidge, 30th president of the United States, was born in Plymouth Notch, Vermont, on July 4, 1872. During his presidency between 1923 and 1929, the country was generally prosperous, but this ended with the stock market crash of 1929. Coolidge was a man of few words and was called "Silent Cal." Much of his term was dominated by gangsters who fought to control the illegal liquor trade that sprang up during Prohibition.

### FALL FESTIVAL

Vermont's Fall Festival celebrates the autumnal transformation of leaf colors. This concert, in an attractive bandstand in Grafton, is typical of the festivities that take place at this time of year. Country fairs and harvest festivals abound in the state, and there are many summer evening open-air band concerts in Vermont towns.

# VIRGINIA

The East Coast state of Virginia was the first permanent British colonial settlement. It was named after Queen Elizabeth I of England, the "Virgin Queen." But it was King James I who approved the setting up of the first colony in Jamestown on May 14, 1607. Since then, the state has played a key role in the nation's development and history. Virginia extends from Chesapeake Bay in the east to the Allegheny Mountains in the west. The land regions are varied and include the Blue Ridge Mountains, the Piedmont Plateau, and the fertile Tidewater areas, where the Potomac, Rappahannock York, and James rivers flow into Chesapeake Bay. The most fertile soil is in the Shenandoah Valley. Skyline Drive, through Shenandoah National Park, offers spectacular panoramic views of the surrounding countryside. Virginia is chiefly an agricultural state, whose main crops are tobacco, peanuts, and tomatoes. Richmond, the capital, is a major producer of cigarettes. Tobacco was first cultivated by white settlers in 1612 from seeds brought from the West Indies by one of the colonists. Because it is located close to Washington, D.C., the nation's capital, Virginia has many federal government buildings and offices providing employment for almost 20 percent of the state's large population.

Virginia has perhaps the greatest number of historical attractions in the United States. To the southeast of Richmond lie Jamestown, site of the first settlement; the restored colonial town of Williamsburg, Virginia's capital between 1699 and 1779; and Yorktown, where the British finally surrendered to the Americans in 1781. Richmond itself was raided by British troops, led by the treacherous Benedict Arnold earlier that year, and some of its buildings were burned. Richmond also served as the capital of the Confederacy during most of the Civil War.

*Dogwood*

*STATE SYMBOLS*

*Cardinal*

*Flowering dogwood*

### ARLINGTON NATIONAL CEMETERY
The Tomb of the Unknowns, where the nation honors its dead from four wars of the 1900s, is at Arlington National Cemetery, Virginia. The tomb itself contains an unidentified World War I soldier. Servicemen from World War II, the Korean War, and the Vietnam War are buried nearby. The cemetery is also the site of this 78-foot (24-m) high bronze statue of U.S. Marines raising the American flag on Iwo Jima Island in the Pacific during World War II. A torch burns night and day over the grave of President John F. Kennedy, who was buried in Arlington in 1963.

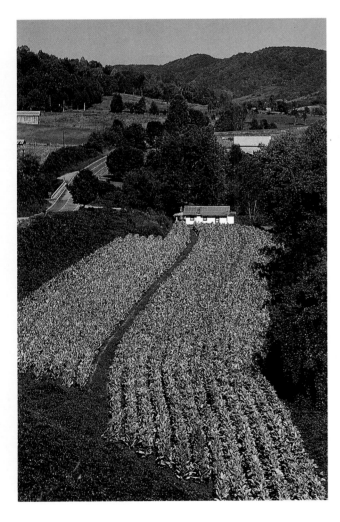

### TOBACCO FIELDS
Shaded valleys, such as this one in Jonesville, Virginia, provide excellent shelter for the state's many tobacco fields. Tobacco, grown in the southern Piedmont, is the chief crop. It was also the earliest colonial crop, first planted by the colony's second leader, John Rolfe, in 1612 near Jamestown. He raised a small crop from seeds he had brought with him from the West Indies. During the 1700s tobacco plantations flourished, as slaves were brought in to work on them.

### MOUNT VERNON
George Washington's home, Mount Vernon near Alexandria, is one of Viginia's major historical landmarks. Some of the trees next to the house were planted by Washington himself. The house has wide, sweeping lawns and well-tended grounds with views over the Potomac River. It was Washington's home from 1754–1799.

## ROCK OF AGES

Natural Bridge, near the border with West Virginia, is a 215-foot (65-m) -high limestone arch. It was once owned by Thomas Jefferson, and George Washington climbed it as a young man to mark his initials on the rock.

### VIRGINIA

**Capital**
Richmond
**Area**
42,774 sq. mi.
(110,776 sq. km)
**Population**
7,712,091 (2007)
**Largest cities**
Virginia Beach (435,619)
Norfolk (238,832)
**Statehood**
June 25, 1788
Rank: 10th
**Principal rivers**
James, Potomac,
Shenandoah
**Highest point**
Mt. Rogers
5,729 feet (1,746m)
**Motto**
*Sic Semper Tyrannis*
(Thus Always to Tyrants)
**Song**
"Carry Me Back to
Old Virginia"

## FIRST PRESIDENT

George Washington, the first U.S. President, was born on February 22, 1732, in Westmoreland County, Virginia. He led the country to victory over British troops in the Revolutionary War. The nation's capital was built near his home in his honor.

## ROBERT E. LEE

Born into an old Virginia family, Robert E. Lee was the leading general of the Confederacy. Lincoln offered him the job of commanding the Union Army at the start of the Civil War in 1861, but Lee turned it down because he could not, he said, raise his hand against his relatives and his home. When Virginia left the Union, Lee joined the Confederacy. He won several important victories against larger, better-equipped Union armies, but eventually he was forced to surrender.

## BLUE RIDGE MOUNTAINS

There is plenty of agricultural land in the rolling Piedmont foothills below the peaks of the Blue Ridge mountains in Virginia. Vast hardwood and conifer forests abound, with cascading streams and rugged cliffs. Wildlife includes bears, deer, bobcats, groundhogs, chipmunks, and 200 species of birds. There are so many types of flowers that they have not yet all been listed. This area attracts many hikers and campers and extends into North Carolina.

# WASHINGTON

Suitably named the "Evergreen State," Washington has large regions covered with beautiful Douglas fir, cedar, and spruce woods. The eastern half of the state, however, is a vast area of dry, flat sagebrush desert reclaimed by irrigation. It is now cattle-grazing and wheat-growing country with a continental climate similar to that of the north-Midwestern states. The Cascade Range effectively splits the state from north to south, with the western portion being lush and green and very wet and cool. About 75 percent of the state's population live in the western region, mostly along the shores of Puget Sound. This is an inlet of the Pacific flanked by the Coast and Cascade mountain ranges. Washington's largest city, Seattle once the main port for Alaska, lies at the mouth of Puget Sound, and the capital, Olympia, lies at the southern tip of Puget Sound on the Olympic Peninsula. Seen on a map, it may not look like a peninsula, but the Olympia area is surrounded by water on three sides. The Olympic Mountain range dominates the peninsula. Captain George Vancouver, a British sea captain, sailed into the Sound in 1792 and claimed the area for Great Britain. Britain and the United States ruled Washington jointly until 1846. Today this Pacific Coast state is bordered on the north by the Canadian province of British Columbia, on the east by Idaho, on the south by Oregon, and on the west by the Pacific Ocean. The Columbia

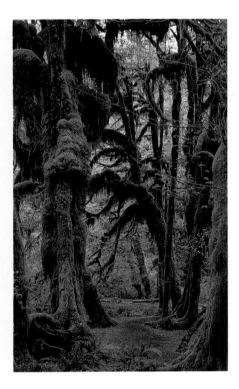

River, which rises in Canada and flows south, is Washington's most important waterway. It is joined by the Snake River as it cuts through eastern Washington and forms the border with Oregon as it bends west. About halfway down its course lies the Grand Coulee Dam, completed in 1942. It is the largest concrete dam in the United States and is also one of the biggest U.S. hydroelectric projects, providing water for the drier eastern part of the state. Washington is second only to Oregon in lumber production. Its forests yield plywood, paper, cardboard, containers, and furniture.

### WASHINGTON

**Capital**
Olympia
**Area**
71,300 sq. mi.
(184,653 sq. km)
**Population**
6,468,424 (2007)
**Largest cities**
Seattle (592,800)
Spokane (204,400)
**Statehood**
November 11, 1889
Rank: 42nd
**Principal rivers**
Columbia, Snake,
Spokane
**Highest point**
Mt. Rainier
14,410 feet (4,395m)
**Motto**
*Alki* (By and By)
**Song**
"Washington,
My Home"

## HALL OF MOSSES
In Olympic National Park on the Olympic Peninsula, lush carpets of fern, mosses, and forest flowers line the rain-soaked forest. After California's Giant Redwood trees, this park's Sitka spruces and Douglas firs are the tallest trees in the United States—many as tall as a 25-story building. During the winter months the forests get as much as 140 inches (356cm) of rain.

### STATE SYMBOLS

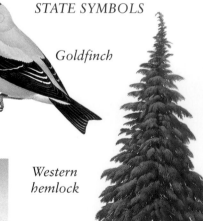

*Goldfinch*

*Western hemlock*

## MT. ST. HELENS
On May 18, 1980, Mt. St. Helens in the Cascade Range erupted with the force of an atomic bomb. The volcano had lain dormant for 123 years. It was the first volcanic eruption in the continental United States since 1917 and by far the most violent. Sixty people were killed by the eruption, and hundreds of miles of surrounding forests were covered with gray ash. The remains of Douglas firs burned and broken by the explosion's force have been left as "exhibits" at a special volcanic monument.

*Coast rhododendron*

## THE APPLE STATE
Washington is the leading apple producer in the United States—especially of the Red and Golden Delicious varieties. The western part of the state has a mild and wet climate that is ideal for growing this fruit.

## SEATTLE
The largest city in Washington, Seattle is a major lumber port and scientific center. The 607-foot (185-m) Space Needle, shown here, is clearly seen by anyone approaching the city by boat on the Puget Sound. It was built for Century 21, the world fair held in Seattle in 1962. The city also boasts a monorail system and other reminders of the fair. These include the Pacific Science Center with its interesting architecture and exhibits, the Opera house, Art pavilion, and award-winning International Fountain.

## MULE DEER
The black-tailed, or mule, deer lives in the western United States, including Washington. Like other deer it feeds on leaves, fruit, grass, and sometimes moss, bark, and twigs—all of which exist in abundance in the western portion of the state. Speed is the deer's main defense against many predators—human and animal. This deer can reach speeds of 30 miles per hour (48km/h).

## WASHINGTON'S PORTS
Tacoma docks seen from an aerial view. Tacoma developed around a sawmill and today is the center of a large forest-products industry. Several ports on Puget Sound have shipbuilding facilities, and there is an enormous amount of trade, both import and export, conducted through such ports as Tacoma and Seattle, with other Pacific Ocean ports, particularly in Asia. There is commercial fishing on Puget Sound.

## BOEING JETS
The metropolitan area of Seattle is the location for several Boeing plants, which turn out aircraft and aerospace equipment. Aircraft manufacturing is a leading industry in Washington. The Boeing Corporation has been making aircraft and aircraft parts there since World War II, when it was the largest employer in the state. The business depends on orders from the U.S. Defense Department and from airlines.

*Boeing 747*

*Boeing KC-135 Stratotanker*

# WEST VIRGINIA

West Virginia was once part of Virginia. It became a state out of the turmoil of the Civil War. In 1861 Virginia voted to withdraw from the Union, but delegates from some of the western counties rebelled against this and set up their own "state," which they called Kanawha. During the war, in 1863 this temporary arrangement was officially accepted by Congress, and West Virginia became the 35th state of the Union.

To the north of West Virginia are Maryland and Pennsylvania, while the western border is with Ohio and Kentucky; Virginia lies to the east and south. West Virginia is nicknamed the "Mountain State" because it has the highest average elevation east of the Mississippi River. Much of West Virginia's land is too rocky for cultivation. It is also fairly isolated from other states and commercial centers by the Appalachian Range, with its thickly wooded slopes, deep gorges, and valleys.

Because of this its people have been faced with many economic problems. After World War II, while the country as a whole enjoyed prosperity, West Virginia suffered a recession. Since the 1950s many West Virginians have left the state. For those who remain to work the land, the best farmland is in the Ohio and Kanawha river valleys. The latter is rich bluegrass country that supports livestock farming. Milk, eggs, and honey are also important farm products. The major West Virginia crops are apples and peaches. Manufacturing is important to the state's economy, especially chemical and metal products. Coal, natural gas, and oil mining are also major industries. The towns of Williamstown and Milton are famous glassmaking centers. Although heavily industrialized, West Virginia also has much unspoiled countryside. Tourism serves as another source of income for the state. Harpers Ferry is a famous historic site, and the mineral springs of White Sulphur Springs and Berkeley Springs have been attracting visitors for over 150 years.

*Sugar maple*

STATE SYMBOLS

*Cardinal*

*Rhododendron*

## A MOUNTAINOUS STATE

The Appalachian Mountains, including the Blue Ridge range, form a high boundary between West Virginia and Virginia and include the state's highest mountain, Spruce Knob. Virtually all of West Virginia is mountainous, and the average elevation of the state is 1,500 feet (450m). This region also includes most of the Potomac River Basin. The area is heavily forested, and the Monongahela National Forest alone covers 1,642,000 acres (665,000 hectares).

## HARPERS FERRY

Standing where the Potomac meets the Shenandoah River, Harpers Ferry is an attractive, historic town and site of the famous event in 1859, when anti-slavery campaigner John Brown seized the U.S. arsenal in a violent attempt to free some slaves. The restored town includes forges, a tavern, a post office, and other buildings of the pre-Civil War years. John Brown was forced to surrender by Lieutenant Colonel Robert E. Lee, and was tried and convicted of treason against Virginia and hanged.

| WEST VIRGINIA | |
|---|---|
| **Capital** | |
| Charleston | |
| **Area** | |
| 24,230 sq. mi. | |
| (62,751 sq. km) | |
| **Population** | |
| 1,812,035 (2007) | |
| **Largest cities** | |
| Charleston (53,421) | |
| Huntington (51,475) | |
| **Statehood** | |
| June 20, 1863 | |
| Rank: 35th | |
| **Principal rivers** | |
| Ohio, Potomac | |
| **Highest point** | |
| Spruce Knob | |
| 4,861 feet (1,483m) | |
| **Motto** | |
| *Montani Semper Liberi* | |
| (Mountaineers Are | |
| Always Free) | |
| **Song** | |
| "The West Virginia Hills" | |

## CHARLESTON
Much of West Virginia's industry is centered around Charleston, the capital and largest city of the state. An impressive State Capitol faces the Kanawha River and also houses a natural history and art museum. Many consumer products such as nylon were developed in the area, and tourists can visit the chemical plants.

## ANCIENT MOUNDS
One of the largest Native American burial mounds is the Grave Creek Mound in the appropriately named Moundsville. A museum contains relics that have been found there of a people dating from the first century B.C. Most of the large mounds were used for burial purposes. Statues such as this have helped archaeologists discover the age and purpose of these mounds.

## COAL MINING
Coal seams run under half of West Virginia, making it the possessor of one of the richest coal deposits in the country. The state ranks as one of the top coal producers in the U.S., second only to Wyoming. Most of the biggest mines are in the southwestern part of the state, where coal was first discovered in 1742. The coal-mining industry has experienced many bitter strikes, in which violence between miners and company guards has taken many lives. Because it is cheap, local coal is used to produce steam and electric power. Coal is also the source of chemicals used in the manufacture of records, cosmetics, and plastics.

## FINGER LAKE
One of the largest lakes in West Virginia, Sutton Lake is a typical finger lake—long and narrow—and lies near the center of the state. The state has many rivers, including the Ohio River, which forms West Virginia's western border, and the Potomac to the northeast.

## COUNTRY MUSIC
There is a strong folk music tradition in the southern Appalachians, especially in West Virginia. Mountain music is played on beautifully crafted musical instruments, such as fiddles, banjos, guitars, and dulcimers, accompanied by singing and dancing.

# WISCONSIN

The north Midwestern state of Wisconsin is almost completely surrounded by water. Lake Michigan lies to the east, the Menominee River to the northeast, Lake Superior forms the northern border, and the St. Croix and Mississippi rivers form the western border. Within the state there are more than 8,000 lakes. The low-lying, rolling plains with their lush pastures are ideal for dairy cattle, and Wisconsin produces much of the nation's milk, cheese, and butter. The state's many farms also grow fruit and vegetables, including corn, peas, tomatoes, cranberries, and cherries. Beef cattle and hogs are raised, especially in the south. Once a major lumber producer, Wisconsin has embarked on a program of forest conservation. Forests cover half the state, the most significant trees being ash, aspen, and elm. The lake port cities are key industrial centers, and fishing in the two Great Lakes is important to the state's industry. Water pollution, however, is a problem.

Wisconsin has hot summers and icy winters, though the weather on the lake shores is milder all year round. The state's main mineral resource is lead, which was mined quite early in its history. Stone is also quarried. Wisconsin's lake shores are favored by travelers and tourists, as are the Chequamegon and Nicolet national forests. The latter is named after Jean Nicolet, a French explorer who was the first to see the Wisconsin area in the 1600s. French fur traders, trappers, and missionaries followed, but the British took control in 1763 after the French and Indian War. Many settlers from the East and immigrants from Europe arrived between 1830 and 1850. Wisconsin joined the Union in 1848.

## WISCONSIN

**Capital**
Madison
**Area**
54,310 sq. mi.
(140,652 sq. km)
**Population**
5,601,640 (2007)
**Largest cities**
Milwaukee (573,358)
Madison (223,389)
**Statehood**
May 29, 1848
Rank: 30th
**Principal rivers**
Wisconsin,
Mississippi,
Chippewa
**Highest point**
Timms Hill
1,951 feet (595m)
**Motto**
Forward
**Song**
"On, Wisconsin!"

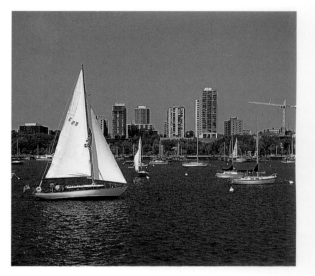

### MILWAUKEE
The largest city in the state, Milwaukee is a busy commercial center in the Midwest. The city is home to many European immigrants, including Poles and Germans. When French fur trappers first arrived there in the 1600s, they heard local Native Americans referring to the place as *Mahn-a-waukee Seepe*, which means "Gathering Place by the River." Milwaukee stands on Lake Michigan, where the Milwaukee and Menominee rivers meet. Its fine harbor is open most of the year and is accessible by the largest ships using the Great Lakes and the St. Lawrence Seaway.

### DAIRY FARMING
After manufacturing, the most important business in Wisconsin is farming. Of the 77,000 farms, over half are geared to dairying, and the state is known as "America's Dairyland." Each October in Madison, the state capital, there is a World Dairy Expo, which features Wisconsin's dairy animals and products. Turkeys, pigs, chickens, and sheep are also raised. Corn, beans, peas, hay, oats, and cabbage are grown.

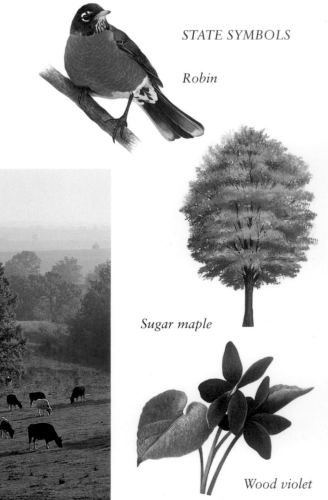

*STATE SYMBOLS*

*Robin*

*Sugar maple*

*Wood violet*

LAKE SUPERIOR

APOSTLE ISLANDS
NAT. LAKESHORE

Superior

Ashland

MICHIGAN

Danbury

CHEQUAMEGON

Webster

Hayward

SUPERIOR    UPLAND

Menominee R.

NICOLET

NAT. FOREST

NAT. FOREST

Ladysmith

△ Timms Hill
1,951 ft (595 m)

Menominee

River Falls

Chippewa Falls

Eau Claire

Wausau

Green Bay

Marshfield

LAKE MICHIGAN

Stevens Point

Green Bay

Wisconsin Rapids

Appleton

90

Oshkosh    Lake
Winnebago    Manitowoc

La Crosse

Wisconsin Dells

Fond du Lac    Sheboygan

Baraboo    Beaver Dam

43

Wisconsin R.

Watertown

Prairie
du Chien

Oconomowoc

Boscobel    Madison    94

Milwaukee

IOWA

Waukesha    Muskego

Lancaster    94

Darlington    Janesville    Racine

Beloit    Elkhorn    Kenosha

ILLINOIS

MINNESOTA

St. Croix R.

Mississippi R.

94

0    100 kilometers
0    50 miles

ORSON WELLES
Born in Wisconsin on May 6, 1915, actor, director, producer, and writer Orson Welles was one of the most influential Americans in the motion picture industry. His film *Citizen Kane* (1941), based on the life of a newspaper tycoon, is considered one of the best movies ever made.

BREWERY
Milwaukee is famous as a beer-producing city. Its beers are canned, bottled, and shipped all over the world. Brewing was started by German immigrants in the 1840s. This is Pabst Brewery, which produces one of the best-known beers in the world. Visitors may tour one of the city's breweries.

BADGERS
Wisconsin's nickname is the "Badger State." During the 1820s a lead boom attracted many miners to the state, who were too busy mining to build houses. Instead they lived in abandoned mine shafts or makeshift burrows. They reminded people of badgers, which use their long claws to dig burrows.

WISCONSIN DELLS
The Wisconsin River winds through the Wisconsin Dells—scenic gorges carved by the river's strong currents. The channel is up to 150 feet (45m) deep. The river starts near the Wisconsin-Michigan border and flows through the center of the state past rapids and the Dells. Tourism is important in this area. The Wisconsin eventually joins the Mississippi River after a course of 430 miles (690km). The river is navigable by small craft for about half its length.

# WYOMING

A land of wide, open spaces, Wyoming ranks in the top-ten states for size but has the smallest population. The state is known for its beautiful mountain scenery and for being the site of the country's oldest national park—Yellowstone.
Over half of Wyoming's land, including Yellowstone, is owned by the U.S. Government, which controls grazing and logging.

The state is a near-perfect rectangle in shape, stretching 367 miles (591km) from east to west and 278 miles (448km) from north to south. There are two main types of terrain: high plains and mountains. This gives Wyoming the second highest overall elevation after Colorado. Even the lowest point is 3,100 feet (945m) above sea level. The mainly arid soil is not particularly fertile, and much of the state's income is derived from oil and oil refining. Cattle ranching is also important, and Wyoming has ten times as many cattle as people.

Apart from Yellowstone National Park and Grand Teton National Park, sightseers can also visit Fort Laramie and Fort Bridger, which were welcome stops for pioneers following the Oregon Trail. Natural wonders include Hell's Half Acre in central Wyoming, a 320-acre (130-hectare) depression filled with caverns; and Devil's Tower, a huge volcanic rock.

French explorers first entered Wyoming in 1743. John Colter, a Virginian, explored the Yellowstone area in 1807. He was part of the Lewis and Clark expedition. Colter stayed on in the region to trap fur animals, and other trappers soon followed. They encountered nomadic Native American tribes—Sioux, Crow, Ute, Bannock, and Arapaho.

As Wyoming was first to grant women the vote, in 1869 it is called the Equality State.

*Cottonwood*

*STATE SYMBOLS*

*Indian paintbrush*

*Western meadowlark*

## YELLOWSTONE NATIONAL PARK

In the northwest corner of Wyoming lie 3,472 square miles (8,992 sq. km) of Yellowstone National Park, which spreads into Montana and Idaho. The park was established in 1872, the first of its kind in the world. Within the park are some 10,000 geysers, hot springs, mud volcanoes, fossil forests, and several canyons and waterfalls, as well as the 1,000-foot (305-m) deep canyon and 308-foot (94-m) high waterfall of the Yellowstone River. A wide variety of animals, including bison, moose, elk, deer, and bighorn sheep, roam freely here in their natural habitat. The park attracts some 2 million visitors each year, creating problems for the ecological balance of the area.

Morning Glory Pool, pictured here, is a hydrothermal pool—one with steam-heated water. Several kinds of algae of different colors grow in water at different temperature levels. The waters are crystal clear, fading into deep aquamarine. Animals are drawn to such thermal pools.

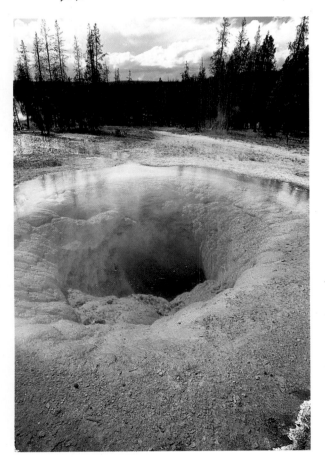

## CATTLE RANCHERS

A young rancher tries his skill at rounding up cattle. Because the soil is so arid and grass so scarce, it takes as many as 50 acres (20 hectares) to feed one cow. Cowboys also perform in the state rodeos. Some work on dude ranches, resorts that offer tourists a flavor of ranch life.

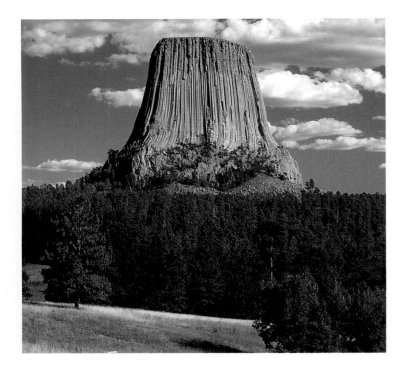

## DEVIL'S TOWER
In northeastern Wyoming stands the impressive Devil's Tower. It was formed by the upsurge of molten lava millions of years ago in the Black Hills. Designated the country's first national monument in 1906, it is a vertical mass of volcanic rock, rising 865 feet (264m) from its base. Many moviegoers will recognize it as inspiring the scene for the spaceship landing in Steven Spielberg's classic science fiction movie, *Close Encounters of the Third Kind* (1977).

## ELK HERDS
North of Jackson Hole is the National Elk Refuge, with a herd of 7,500 elk. The elk gather there in winter for feeding, pawing through the snow to reach the dense grasses on the plains. Visitors can take a supervised sleigh ride through the herd.

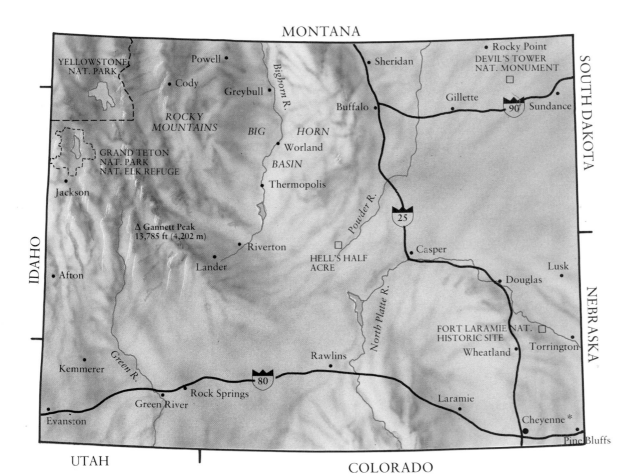

## OIL DRILLING
Wyoming ranks tenth in the United States in mineral production. The chief industry is oil refining. Here, oil workers use the heavy drills to extract more of this precious commodity. Wyoming has vast reserves of other energy-producing minerals. Because it is also a major producer of hydroelectric power, it exports power to other states.

## NELLIE TAYLOE ROSS
The first female governor in the United States was Nellie Tayloe Ross. She was elected to succeed her late husband as governor of Wyoming in 1924, 16 days before another woman governor was elected in Texas. She was later appointed director of the U.S. Mint—making her one of the first women in the United States to also hold such an important federal post.

# OUTLYING U.S. AREAS

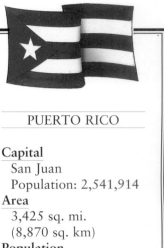

Apart from the 50 states and the District of Columbia, which make up the United States, there is one Caribbean commonwealth and a number of Pacific islands and atolls with U.S. assistance agreements. This means that they come under U.S. protection and receive U.S. financial and military assistance. More importantly for the islanders, it means they are all U.S. citizens, although they cannot vote in U.S. presidential elections when living in the territories. Of these outlying U.S. areas, the single largest and most important is the Commonwealth of Puerto Rico. It consists of beautiful islands lying between the Atlantic Ocean to the north and the Caribbean Sea to the south, 1,040 miles (1,673km) southwest of Miami, Florida. Each year around five million tourists enjoy Puerto Rico's sandy beaches and pleasant mild climate, with a mean temperature of 77° F (25°C). Tourism earns the island almost $2 billion every year.

Christopher Columbus landed on the island in 1493 at a time when the Arawak people inhabited the land. It is believed to be the only part of the United States where Columbus ever set foot. The U.S. took control of the island from Spain following the Spanish-American War of 1898, and it became a commonwealth in 1952. Most of the residents still speak Spanish as their first language.

The second-largest U.S. territory after Puerto Rico is Guam, one of the Mariana Islands. The Federated States of Micronesia, Marshall Islands, and Palau were all formerly U.N. Trust Territories under U.S. administration. They have all gained independence but maintain a "Compact of Free Association" with the U.S. This means that the U.S. Government continues with financial and/or governmental assistance.

## PUERTO RICO

**Capital**
San Juan
Population: 2,541,914
**Area**
3,425 sq. mi.
(8,870 sq. km)
**Population**
3,941,459 (2007)
**Principal river**
Arecibo
**Highest point**
Cerro de Punta
4,390 feet (1,339m)
**Motto**
*Joannes Est Nomen Eius* (John Is His Name)
**Song**
*"La Borinqueña"*

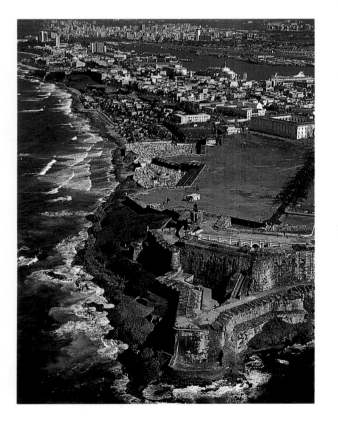

### BANANAS
About 70 percent of Puerto Rico's land is farmland, and bananas are the major fruit crop. Bananas and plantains, which are starchy fruits similar to bananas, are grown inland in most regions of the island. Exotic fruits such as papayas and star apples are also cultivated.

### PUERTO RICO
The first Spanish settlement on the island was built in 1509 following the conquest of the island by the Spanish explorer Ponce de León. It was situated in Caparra, across the bay from the capital, San Juan, pictured here. The island's income used to come from trade in slaves, gold, and sugar cane.

PUERTO RICO

Isabela
Aguadilla
Arecibo
San Juan *
Vega Baja
Carolina
Luquillo
Bayamón
Guaynabo
Mayagüez
Caguas
Fajardo
Sabana Grande
Δ Cerro de Punta 4,389 ft (1,339 m)
Juana Díaz
Humaco
Ponce
Guayama

VIRGIN ISLANDS (U.S.)

St. Thomas I.
Dewey
Charlotte *
Amalie
St. John I.
*Isla de Culebra*
Isabel Segunda
*Isla de Vieques*
St. Croix I.

### DUGOUT CANOES
Ocean-going dugout canoes with outriggers ply the Pacific islands. Many, such as these, are converted for sailing, with a single canvas sail. Some fishing is done from these canoes.

### GUAM
The largest and southernmost of the Mariana Islands, Guam, is a U.S. territory. It is known as the place "Where America's day begins," because it lies west of the International Date Line. Guam is 210 square miles (541 sq. km) in size. It has a large U.S. air base that was important during the Vietnam War.

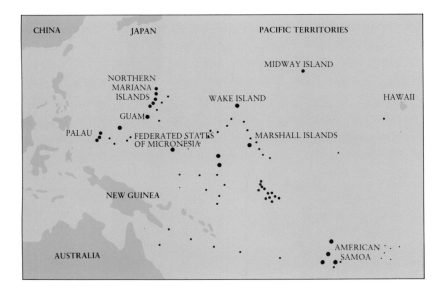

PACIFIC TERRITORIES

CHINA
JAPAN
MIDWAY ISLAND
NORTHERN MARIANA ISLANDS
WAKE ISLAND
HAWAII
GUAM
PALAU
FEDERATED STATES OF MICRONESIA
MARSHALL ISLANDS
NEW GUINEA
AMERICAN SAMOA
AUSTRALIA

### SAMOAN HOUSE
American Samoans make their stilted houses from the local materials on the islands, such as coconut tree trunks and fronds. The people are of Polynesian origin, like those of Hawaii, and work and live in family and village groups. American Samoa is made up of six islands and is the most southerly of all lands under U.S. sovereignty. Most inhabitants live in and around Pago Pago on Tutuila Island.

### VIRGIN ISLANDS
Charlotte Amalie is the capital of the American Virgin Islands, which consist of St. Thomas, St. John, and St. Croix. The islands lie 70 miles (113km) east of Puerto Rico. Charlotte Amalie, on St. Thomas, is a major port. Its main industries include tourism, rum, textiles, perfumes, and watches.

### COFFEE BEANS
Coffee competes with sugar cane as the most valuable crop of Puerto Rico. It is grown in the western part of the central mountains. This picture shows a coffee plant with clusters of ripening fruit. The fruit is red and is called a cherry. Each cherry contains two beans which are roasted, ground, and sold to make into the drink called coffee.

### CARNIVAL
The original Spanish influence still pervades many of Puerto Rico's festivals and celebrations. Each town has a patron saint, and saints' days are celebrated with music festivals and carnivals such as this. The largest festival is in San Juan in the summer. It was once directed by the island's most famous resident, the cellist Pablo Casals.

121

# FACTS AND FIGURES

MT. McKINLEY
The highest mountain in the United States is Mt. McKinley in Alaska.

REDWOOD TREES
The tallest trees in the United States are the giant redwoods of California.

FAULT LINE
The San Andreas fault stretches 750 miles (1,200km) north to south in California.

**UNITED STATES FACTS**
Total area of the United States 3,717,810 sq. miles (9,628,384 sq. km)

**Widest point**
From coast to coast (excluding Hawaii and Alaska) the United States Measures 2,807 miles (4,519km)

**Highest point**
Mt. McKinley, Alaska 20,320 feet (6,194m)

**Lowest point**
Death Valley, California 282 feet (86km) below sea level

**Highest state**
Colorado, average mean elevation, 6,800 feet (2,070m)

**Lowest state**
Delaware, average mean elevation, 60 feet (18m)

**Northernmost point**
Point Barrow, Alaska

**Southernmost point**
Ka Lae, Hawaii

**Easternmost point**
Pochnoi Point, Alaska

**Westernmost point**
Amatignak Island, Alaska

**Largest lakes**
Superior, 31,820 sq. miles (88,016 sq. km)
Huron, 23,010 sq. miles (82,414 sq. km)
Michigan, 22,400 sq. miles (59,596 sq. km)

**Longest rivers**
Mississippi, 2,340 miles (3,766km)
Missouri, 2,315 miles (3,725km)
Rio Grande, 1,760 miles (2,830km)
Arkansas, 1,459 miles (2,348km)
Colorado, 1,450 miles (2,333km)

**Coastline**
The United States has 12,383 miles (19,937km) of coastline

**Geographic center**
48 states: near Lebanon, Kansas; all 50 states: Butte County, South Dakota

**Highest human settlement**
Climax, Colorado, 11,360 feet (3,526m), well over 2 miles (3km) high

**Lowest human settlement**
Calipatria, California, 184 feet (56m) below sea level

**Largest national park**
Wrangell-St. Elias, Alaska, 13,018 sq. miles (33,717 sq. km)

**Tallest structure**
A TV tower in Blanchard, North Dakota, 2,063 feet (629m) high

**Highest bridge**
Royal Gorge, in Colorado, 1,053 feet (321m) above water

**Tallest building**
Sears Tower, Chicago, Illinois, 1,454 feet (443m) high

KODIAK BEAR
The largest bear in the United States and the world is the Kodiak bear from Alaska.

CHICAGO GIANT
The Sears Tower in Chicago rises 110 stories, dominating the city's skyline along the shores of Lake Michigan.

L.A. SMOG
The worst air pollution in the United States occurs in the Greater Los Angeles area.

# Map Index

# General Index

## PHOTOGRAPHIC ACKNOWLEDGMENTS

The publishers wish to thank Zefa for supplying most of the photographs inside this book. Additional photographs were supplied by:

**Allsport:** 53 top; Paul Bahn: 101 center left; **Associated Press/Topham:** 108 bottom right; **Gary A.M. Browne:** 22 bottom; **J. Allan Cash:** 8 bottom, 13 top right, 21 bottom right, 26 bottom, 43 top, 60 left, 65 bottom, 67 top, 73 top left, 98 top, 111 top; **Bruce Coleman Ltd:** 12 top, 42 top, 119 top, 120 right, 121 top right and center left; **Colorsport:** 47 top; **Dermot Curnyn:** 31 top left; **Delaware State Travel and Tourism Dept.:** 35 center; **Michael Dent:** 114 center left; **Lawrence Englesberg:** 11 center; **Mary Evans Picture Library:** 33 bottom center, 57 bottom right, 77 middle; **Eye Ubiquitous:** 76 bottom right; **Ronald Grant Archive:** 117 top; **Susan Griggs Agency:** 7 top and bottom, 8 top, 10 bottom, 49 top, 51 center left and bottom left, 53 center and center right, 55 bottom, 65 top and center, 71 bottom, 78 top, 95 top right, 109 center, 115 top right, 118 bottom right; **Robert Harding Picture Library:** 14 top, 15 bottom, 29 center left, 31 center right, 38 bottom right, 39 bottom left, 52 bottom, 56 bottom left, 75 center left, 77 bottom, 80 top and bottom, 89 center, 96 bottom, 97 center, 107 bottom, 110 bottom left and bottom right, 111 bottom, 121 top left; **Grant Heilman:** 27 top left, 30 bottom, 35 top, 39 bottom right, 43 bottom, 48 bottom, 67 bottom, 73 top right, 75 bottom, 90 top, 116 bottom; **Hulton Picture Company:** 20 bottom left, 21 bottom left, 28 right, 40 right, 51 center right, 58 center, 68 left, 89 bottom left, 90 bottom right, 100 center, 119 bottom center; **The Hutchison Library:** 33 bottom, 91 center, 115 bottom; **The Image Bank:** 17 top left, 56 bottom right, 69 bottom; **Kos Photos/Sharon Green:** 97 top; **Magnum:** 89 bottom right (Erich Hartman); **NAACP:** 39 bottom center; **New Jersey Dept. of Travel and Tourism:** 78 bottom left; **Peter Newark Pictures:** 54 bottom, 59 top center, 66 bottom, 91 bottom; **Photo Researchers Inc.:** 53 bottom left, 115 top left; **Popperfoto:** 45 bottom; **Range/Bettmann/UPI** 24 top left, 27 top right, 60 top left, 62 middle, 66 top, 70 top, 79 top left, 85 middle, 88 bottom left; **Science Photo Library:** 99 top; **Sefton Photo Library:** 55 top; **Phil Sheldon Golf Picture Library:** 99 right; **Stockmarket:** 20 bottom, 93 top; **Tony Stone Worldwide:** 17 bottom left, 21 top, 23 top right, 26 top, 27 center, 35 bottom, 44 bottom, 57 top, 58 bottom, 62 bottom, 68 right, 72 top, 77 top, 85 top, 96 top, 100 top, 109 bottom, 116 top, 117 center and bottom, 121 bottom right; **Topham Picturepoint:** 92 bottom; **TRIP:** 83 top (R. Fairer-Smith), 105 top (I. Mitchell); **Valan Photos:** 79 top right; **West Virginia Government Office:** 115 center; **Wichita Art Museum:** 95 bottom left.